WILD PRESERVES

Illustrated Recipes for over 100 Natural Jams and Jellies

STONE WALL PRESS, INC.
1241 30th Street N.W.
Washington, D.C. 20007

Disclaimer

The facts and opinions expressed herein are solely those of the author. Neither the Author nor the Publisher can be held responsible for the mistaken identity of any plant listed in this book.

Library of Congress Card No. 77-10287

ISBN 0-913276-22-7

First Printing August 1977
Second Printing June 1981

To Euell Gibbons

Who made the world a better place to live.
Whose love of nature and its plentiful bounty,
gave us a renewed interest in natural foods.
Whose name and place in history is forever.

FROM THE AUTHOR

Many other cookbooks carry a chapter or section on how to prepare jellies and other preserves. Some cookbooks deal specifically with the preparation of jams and jellies. My concern in this book is to present a practical approach to preserving edible wild fruit, an abundant and tasty natural resource. Perhaps this book will open up a new gastronomic world for you. A world of tasty and nutritious jellies, jams, preserves, conserves, marmalades, butters, and wines.

For many years I have prepared various jellies and other preserves from wild fruit. This has forced me to experiment with many household cookbooks and wild foods cookbooks in order to adopt final recipes. This small book is a combination of plant identification, to help you locate the wild edibles, and recipes for making jellies, jams, and preserves from these wild fruits. The drawings and plant descriptions will serve as a handy reference as you go about the countryside, foraging for ripe wild fruit.

You will notice that basic recipes for jellies and jams occasionally repeat themselves on various pages. Often there are slight variations. This will allow you to continue working without having to flip pages back and forth in order to refer to other parts of the book. A convenience that I am sure you will greatly appreciate.

Where the fruit from a particular plant genus is similar within the species, I have treated them as one. However, in the case of the Viburnums, I have separated most of them because of differences in treatments of quantity, taste, pectins, etc.

HOW TO PREPARE JAMS AND JELLIES

The making of jelly, jam, or preserves offers both men and women an opportunity to be highly creative, for this is not specifically women's work. I, myself, greatly enjoy experimenting with fruit combinations, colors, and flavors.

Jellied fruits have long been the pride of farm women, often winning blue ribbons at country fairs and club shows. This tradition lingers today and jellies and jams continue to be an important aspect of these events. Jellies, jams, preserves, conserves, marmalades, and butters can add zest and a touch of color to a meal. Dwell on the thought of homemade wild blueberry jam on hot toast on a frosty winter morning—a touch of summer splashed against the frigid winter. And the flavor of your colorful jam is always enhanced by the knowledge that you made it yourself.

Making jellies and jams is an excellent way of utilizing the abundance of wild fruits that abound in your area. Irregularly shaped or bruised fruit can be used despite its outward appearance. Many people hesitate to use such misshapen or bruised fruit because they are used to eating only store-bought, quality foodstuffs. In jam making, however, the fruit is reduced to a common pulp by the cooking process. It all tastes great in the end.

Jellies, jams, and preserves are basically alike—that is, acid fruit preserved by means of granulated sugar and cooked in order to provide some degree of jell.

Terms:

Jelly. Made from the acid juice of fruit. When cooked with granulated sugar, the final product is translucent, and will hold its shape. Good jelly quivers and can be cut with a knife.

Jam. Made from crushed fruit and often contains the skins of the fruit. When cooked with granulated sugar, it has a jelly-like consistency, but will not hold its shape.

6

Preserves. Whole or chopped fruit cooked in a thick sugar syrup. It may or may not jell. Fruit can be preserved by one of several methods: by cooking it in a syrup, by sugaring the prepared fruit, by allowing it to stand in a sugar and juice mixture, or by first preparing a sugar and water syrup that is then poured over the fruit. This is one of the simplest methods of storing fruit.

Conserves. A blend of more than one fruit—generally prepared like jam. They may contain a variety of condiments, such as nuts and raisins.

Marmalade. Generally considered to be a special type of jam. It is usually made with citrus fruit such as oranges, lemons, kumquats and grapefruit. The entire fruit may be used, excluding the seeds if there are any.

Butters. Made from blenderized or puréed fruits that are cooked for a considerable length of time in order to obtain a very smooth consistency. Often the unused pulp of jelly making can be made into an excellent butter. Butters frequently rely on the taste of the fruit rather than the sweetness of added sugar.

It is unwise to assume that all wild or commercial fruits have the necessary properties needed to produce good quality jellies or jams. Recipes that come with canning jars or pectin products give only general instructions as to basic technique and necessary ingredients.

There are differences in all food products. Wild fruits may or may not be more acid than commercial varieties and the level of acidity is an important factor in good jelly making. Most recipes in standard cookbooks are based on the predictable range of fruit PH, acid base, size, pulp content and quantity of juice found in commercial fruit. These often differ dramatically in wild, as opposed to commercial fruit, and attempts to adapt these recipes may end in failure. This book is a collection of workable recipes geared specifically for use with **wild** fruits.

There are a few basic rules that one must abide by, and if followed a whole new vista of food preparation is at hand. Remember, however, these rules are basically written down here for application to wild fruits. If adapted to the more well-known commercial species, you may encounter dismal failure.

1. Not all wild fruit contains natural pectin.

2. Wild fruits that contain natural pectin may have varying concentrations.

3. Fruit that is underripe usually jells best; therefore, it is wise to use a combination of underripe and fully ripened fruit. Fully ripened fruit provides a rich flavor.

4. The best quality jelly, jams, etc. is made by preparing small batches at a time.

5. Use required amounts of water in the cooking process, as water dilutes color and flavor.

6. If you use water that has a high chemical concentration, such as chlorine, it will flavor your final product. Either boil out the chlorine or purchase good de-mineralized water.

7. Do not boil juice, pulp or fruit unnecessarily—make it quick and short.

8. Always utilize sterile, hot jars in the final steps.

9. Always store your completed product in a cool, dark storage area. Direct sun destroys color and often upsets the jell consistency.

About Pectins:

Most individuals go about the jelly and jam making process without any real knowledge of the use and chemistry of pectin.

Pectin is a name given to a group of plant substances which under certain conditions will form gels. Pectins serve as binder material for plant cells and are therefore found in practically all types of plant growth, especially in fruits.

Chemically, pectin is a mixture of a very complex carbohydrate substance, araban and pectic acid. The pectic acid is extracted using alcohol, leaving behind the araban. Pectin, because of its stable jelling property, is therefore of considerable nutritional value as it permits the storage of fruit as jellies and jams.

Commercial pectin is usually produced from the peels of citrus fruit and apple pomace, that is the pulp of the apple. It is sold either as a powder or a liquid and it usually has a yellow-white color.

Many fruits lack pectin in sufficient concentrations to effectively yield a gel. Others such as apples, grapes, currants and plums are high in concentration and yield excellent gels.

Fruits high in natural pectin:

Apples, all types	Grapes (underripe)
Barberry	Irish Moss
Blackberry (underripe)	Mountain Ash
Carrion Flower Berry	Oregon Grape
Crab Apple	Plums
Cranberry (Bog)	Thornapple
Currants	

Fruits low in natural pectin:

Bearberry	Mulberries
Blackberry (ripe)	Nannyberry
Black Gum	Papaw
Black Haws	Peppermint
Blueberry	Persimmon
Buffalo Berry	Raspberry
Canada Mayflower	Rhododendron
Cherries	Rhubarb
Choke Pears	Rose Hips
Crowberry	Salal
Elderberries	Sapphireberry
False Solomon's Seal	Sassafras
Ground Cherry	Serviceberry
Hackberry	Snowberry
Hobblebush	Strawberry
Honeylocust	Sumac
Honesuckles	Violets
Indian Cherry	Virginia Creeper
Manzanita	Wintergreen

Using Natural Pectins:

If there is not a suitable concentration of natural pectin in a particular wild fruit, it can be combined with another wild fruit that is rich in pectin. Often proper picking will insure a sufficient concentration of pectin. For example, fully ripened blackberries do not have a sufficient concentration of natural pectin. On the other hand, if you pick 10–20% partially ripened (the berries will be red in color) fruit, there will be enough natural pectin to produce a good gel. All fruits contain less pectin when fully ripened.

The alternative is to combine the main fruit with an appropriate amount of apple peel juice, plum juice or some similar fruit that contains high concentrations of pectin.

How to test for Natural Pectins:

Cook a cupful of the desired fruit juice. Extract one tablespoon of the cooked juice. Place the spoonful of juice into a small glass dish, add one tablespoon of alcohol and mix slowly. Grain alcohol is preferred as denatured or wood alcohol is highly poisonous. If you use denatured or wood alcohol, **DO NOT TASTE THE MIXTURE.**

1. Juices that contain high concentrations of pectin will form large amounts of jelly matter.

2. Juices that contain only moderate concentrations of pectin will form smaller, dispersed amounts of jelly material.

3. Juices low in pectin will yield very small amounts of flaky particles of jelly material.

Another simple test uses Epsom Salts. Commercial Epsom Salts will do. Mix one teaspoonful of Epsom Salts with one tablespoonful of cooked fruit juice in a small glass dish. Mix thoroughly, then allow to stand for 20 minutes. If the cooked fruit juice contains enough pectin it will form a semi-solid or gel mass.

There are several other methods that can be used in the determination of specific concentrations of fruit pectin, but these are long and involved. The methods mentioned above determine general levels, but not specific concentrations, i.e. milligrams of pectin per liter of fruit juice.

Using Commercial Pectins:

Commercial pectins are generally produced in two forms, a thick liquid (such as Certo) or in a powder or granular form. Liquid pectin is added to boiling fruit juice and sugar mixture. Powdered or granular pectin is mixed with unheated fruit juice. I prefer the liquid pectin because it handles easily. You can time the cooking process to produce a cooked product as well as making it the last step in that process. All recipes in this test that mention commercial pectin refer to liquid pectin for these reasons.

The use of natural pectins requires a slightly longer cooking time and requires less sugar per cup of wild fruit juice. The yield of desired jelly per cup of juice is less than when commercial pectin is added.

Jelly or jam that is made with commercial pectin requires less cooking time and less energy to produce. However, more granulated sugar is required with the use of commercial pectin.

Use of Sugar:

Granulated sugar or honey helps in the gel formation. It sweetens and flavors the jelly or jam and acts as a preserving agent. It also helps to firm the tissues of the ripened fruit. Granulated sugar and sugar beet sugar are actually the same although derived from different sources. Corn syrup and honey can also be used as replacements for granulated sugar. If you can hunt up recipes used during W.W.II, you will find corn syrup was utilized as a substitute for the scarce granulated sugar.

Many individuals have given serious thought to finding a workable alternative to granulated sugar. Health and medical officials cite the role of sugar in tooth decay, coronary diseases, diabetes and many other serious problems. For these reasons and others, some individuals substitute honey for sugar. It does contain many original vitamins and minerals. There are as many opinions and methods employed for using honey in the making of jellies and jams as there are perhaps people who make jellies

11

and jams. Whatever you decide, one thing is certain, it requires a lot more time and energy. Cooking time is longer and these recipes will also require the addition of commercial type pectins.

Acids:

High acid content in the wild fruit is required in order for the gel stage to set up and to enhance the flavor. Usually the acid concentration varies in different fruits as well as within the same fruit. Acid content is somewhat higher in slightly ripened fruit than in fully ripened fruit. Fruits may well be rich in natural pectins but lack in sufficient concentrations of fruit acids to yield a good flavor or jelly.

If the fruit or juice utilized is tart, then there should be a sufficient concentration of acid. If fruit acids appear to be lacking, then substitute similar fruit acids. Most cooks prefer lemon juice, but apple juice may also be used. Commercial citric acid can also be purchased from your local druggist or apothecary as a substitute for lemon juice. It is customary to add 1/8 teaspoonful of crystal citric acid in place of each tablespoonful of lemon juice.

Cooking Methods:

Several methods are used to make jellies and jams. Two of the most basic are the cook-down method and the sugar-juice combination. The cook-down is the traditional method, which is the practice of cooking the fruit juice until it becomes fairly concentrated. However, prolonged cooking time reduces the gelling power of the natural pectin and the flavor is reduced as well as the color. A minimum of water is used in order to reduce the juice-concentration and time of cooking.

If you employ the cook-down method, be certain to use fruit that has good concentrations of pectin. A good batch of fruit should contain 20—30% partially ripened fruit for high pectin concentration and the rest, fully ripened for fine flavor.

A much faster method is to combine the granulated sugar with the fruit juice before cooking. This not only reduces the cooking time but also reduces destruction of the pectin. It must also be pointed out that this quick method involves the addition of commercial pectin as it does not allow sufficient time to extract the natural pectins from the fruit.

12

Uncooked or raw jam is perhaps the quickest method employed today. As there are no bacteria destroyed in a cooking process, these fruit preserves must be kept under constant refrigeration. They should be made in small batches and stored for only a few weeks at a time. I recommend the uncooked or raw jam method be used when you utilize delicate fruit such as wild strawberries. The cooking process actually destroys the delicate structure and flavor of this delicious fruit and it will not yield high quality jams. It is best preserved as an uncooked jam and used within a short time to insure its delicious flavor.

Equipment:

A good cook knows that the correct sized kettle, spoon, dish, etc. all help in bringing that jelly or jam to the point of polished perfection. So, before you rush to the cooking area, please select the proper cooking utensils.

A large, heavy saucepan is essential. An 8 or 10 quart saucepan will allow the fruit mixture to come to a full boil without boiling over. A measuring cup with clearly visible markings is important—you don't want to lose time in trying to figure out each measure. A good, clean wooden spoon for stirring and tasting. A food or potato masher, food mill, utility or paring knives, ladle, grater (if required), bowls (stainless or glass) and certainly an accurate clock or timer. A good candy thermometer can be an aid, but not a necessity.

Last but not least, the jelly bag. This is required for extracting fruit juices for jellies. Commercial jelly bags are easily purchased or you may easily make one from several layers of cheesecloth or unbleached muslin. I prefer and use a bleached and washed white cotton sock. It does not matter if the heel is reinforced with nylon. I make up my jellies in small 4 pint batches and the sock is ideal for straining the juices from the fruit pulp. Appalling! No, not as long as you use clean, bleached white socks. They are colorful afterwards, but not recommended for wearing as the natural food colors will leach out.

Containers:

The most common method of sealing jelly jars has been with paraffin. The problem is that you may only seal jellies with paraffin when they are firm; otherwise the paraffin will not provide an even seal. Paraffin, therefore, works well with good jellies and jams but will not provide a good seal for butters, marmalades, preserves and conserves.

The solution to this problem is to use canning jars with rubberized metal seals. These can be used for almost every form of canning or preserving. They are available as jelly or jam jars with colorful decorations and come in several sizes. The jars are reuseable; all that needs to be renewed is the seal. They are time savers in that the time consumed in handling hot paraffin is eliminated.

The jelly jars should be ready before you start to make your delightful jellies or jams. Check the top edge of the jars for cracks and nicks. Anything that impairs a good seal will spoil the jellied product. The jars should be washed in hot soapy water and rinsed well to remove all traces of soap. Never assume that jars are clean—always assume jars are laden with bacteria— wash them.

If the jars are to be filled immediately with boiling hot foods, scald rinse them in boiling hot water and let them stand in the hot rinse water while they wait. The jars should be hot when they are filled. Cool glassware often cracks when suddenly filled with boiling hot food.

Most cooks prefer to sterilize the clean jars by covering them with water and boiling them for ten minutes. Leave them in the hot water until you are ready to use them. Again, this will keep them from cracking, and will keep the insides moist which helps in the setting of the gel.

All lids and rimbands of all types should also be kept hot and sterile, but DO NOT BOIL RUBBERS OR SELF-SEALING LIDS WITH GASKETS along with your jars. This will impair their ability to seal. Instead, put them in a bowl, cover them with boiling water, and let them stand in it until you are ready to use them.

Sterility is perhaps the magic ingredient that usually goes unmentioned. If you use a funnel, it should also be sterile. Sterility of your containers and cookware will insure an enduring product.

A Word About Paraffin:

If you use paraffin to seal jelly or jam jars, it should be poured

14

as soon after the sauce has been poured as possible. About one-eighth of an inch of hot paraffin will provide a layer sufficient to form a good seal. The hot jar will help seal the paraffin at the edges, but twirl the glass container so that there is an even distribution at the sides of the glass. Once this thin layer has set, pour in a second somewhat thicker layer to seal the container completely. Paraffin allows you to use jars of various shapes and mouth widths. Allow the paraffin in wide mouth jars a little more time to thicken than in smaller mouthed jars.

When melting paraffin blocks, use a double boiler. Pour only clear, hot paraffin. As soon as the paraffin has thickened and the jars have cooled enough to handle, they may be stored until used.

The Cooking Process:

Whenever you make a jelly or jam product, with or without added pectin, only prepare small amounts. If you have all the proper preparation materials to handle larger amounts of cooked fruit as well as an appropriate recipe, then the advice given here certainly does not apply. Do not double or triple recipes. It is wise to observe, that even experienced cooks, who have prepared jellies and jams for many years, only prepare small batches at a time.

The amounts of fruits indicated in each of the recipes is approximate as the exact amount will vary with size and juiciness of a particular fruit. The weight or volume stated is needed to yield a given amount of juice called for in the recipe.

All fruit should be stemmed, that is all stems and other debris removed. Wash in cold running water; do not allow to stand in water, this may ruin the firmness of the fruit. Washing will remove any airborne grime as well as other chemical agents that might possibly be present. If you have gathered your fruit near a busy highway there exists the possibility of automobile exhaust products coating the skin of the fruit. Some of these products may not be water soluble, but they can be removed by briskly rubbing the fruit under cold, running tapwater.

Juice from the fruit can be extracted in a number of different ways. Each recipe will indicate the method best suited to each fruit. Tight skinned or firm fruits may have to be heated in order to start the flow of juices, and a very small amount of what is called "cooking" water is usually added. The actual length of cooking time required to extract the fruit juice may differ depending on the ripeness of the individual fruit.

If you are going to make jelly; then you will want to use clear, free of pulp, fruit juice. Place the cooked juicy pulp into a damp jelly bag and allow it to drip freely into a stainless steel or glass container. The clearest jelly is obtained when the juice is allowed to drip without pressure on the bag. The yield is far less than that which is obtained by pressing or squeezing. Pressing or squeezing will force pulp through the pores of the bag. A second straining will remove most of the pulp and provide you with a final clarified juice. Use natural or commercial pectin as indicated in your recipe.

The biggest problem in making jelly is telling when it is done. When you use pectin, there is no problem, as the gel process will follow. It is when you use the cooked-down process depending on natural pectin that you may run into difficulties. In this case, it is important to remove the jelly or jam mixture from the heat before it becomes overcooked. You certainly will know if the jelly or jam has been overcooked as it will exhibit a change in color, odor, taste and smell of burnt or caramelized sugar.

There are three time-proven tests that can aid you in taking your jelly or jam off the heat before it overcooks.

Sheet Test:

The spoon or sheet test is perhaps the oldest and widest in use, even today. Dip a cool metal teaspoon into the hot jelly as it is cooking. Remove the spoon from the mixture and hold it above the pot, away from the steam. Turn the spoon so that the syrup runs off the side. If the jelly flows off the side of the spoon in a "sheet"—consider it done. Note the drawings.

"Sheeting"

"Dropping"

16

The use of the sheet or spoon test requires some skill and experience and it is not always dependable. Keep in mind that if you use honey the jelly product will be somewhat softer.

Temperature Test:

A candy thermometer is a handy device, but a deep fat or an actual jelly thermometer can be just as handy. Take the temperature of boiling water before cooking the jelly. Then cook the jelly mixture until it reaches a temperature of 8° F higher than the temperature of boiling water. This of course will vary according to altitude in the United States.

The concentration of the cooked sugar will be such, at that point, that the mixture will form a satisfactory gel. Be certain that the bulb of your thermometer is completely covered with jelly in order to obtain a good reading.

Refrigeration Test:

Place half of a teaspoonful of the boiling jelly on a chilled plate and put it in the freezer compartment of your refrigerator for 2 minutes. If the mixture gels, then your jelly is ready and can be poured into the hot, sterile jars.

Failures?

There are many reasons why you may experience a failure with the final jelly product. There may be one or more contributing factors, especially when you are first adventuring into preserving wild fruits which are not as predictable as commercially grown fruits.

If jelly or jam jars are improperly sealed, mold may develop, and if yeast gets in, fermentation will result. The taste, consistency, and color will change if preserves are stored for too long a period. Bright red fruits, such as wild strawberries, raspberries and cranberries, fade very easily if left in prolonged sunlight.

If you do not constantly stir your preserves, you may find an improper mixture or fruit that floats at the top of the jars. Also be very certain to skim off as much of the foam that forms during the boiling process as possible. The foam consists of air trapped in the hot juices and it can only be removed by skimming the surface with a large spoon.

17

It is also wise to use only glass or stainless steel cookware. I have done some cooking in aluminum and other types of cookware and found that they tend to give a metallic flavor to jelly or preserves. I prefer stainless steel.

THE RECIPES

CONTENTS

The following edible wild fruit are listed alphabetically for your convenience.

Barberry

BARBERRY
(Berberis sp.)

There are several species of Barberry available throughout the United States both as native and ornamental shrubs. In recent years many varieties have been imported by nursery stockmen.

As a native shrub *(Berberis canadensis)*, it can be found growing wild from New England south along the Appalachian mountains to Georgia and west to Texas. A low shrub, it attains a height of 1–5 feet and thrives in open fields.

European Barberry *(B. vulgaris)* and Japanese Barberry *(B. thunbergii)* are widely used as hedge shrubs because they tolerate close pruning. These three species produce yellow flowers that later in the summer yield scarlet berries. They also bear sharp thorns on each branch. The berries when ripe have a delightful tart flavor and are slightly acid. They usually grow in great abundance on each branch.

Oregon Grape *(B. aquifolium)* is an evergreen barberry that is native to the west coast of Oregon and California. These berries are blue and have a tart, slightly acid flavor. All of the barberries used as ornamentals produce an abundance of fruit that is quite edible. The fruit can be found on the plants throughout the winter months, although it is quite pulpy. The fruit should be picked either in early September or just after the first frost. The berries are tart and you will have to adjust the amount of sugar called for in each of the recipes, according to your tastes. Barberries contain natural pectin; therefore you will not have to add any.

Red Barberry Jelly

> 8 cups ripened barberries
> 1½ cups granulated sugar to each cup of juice
> 1 cup of water

Select the berries carefully, using only fully ripened fruit. Wash and stem the fruit and measure 8 cups. Place the selected fruit into a saucepan and mash them completely. Add 1 cup of cold water. Cook over moderate heat until the juice starts to flow. This may take as long as 10 minutes.

Strain the juice through a jelly bag. For each cup of juice add 1½ cups of granulated sugar. Place the juice in a deep saucepan, mix in the sugar and place over a high heat. Bring to a boil and hold at a boil for 15 minutes or until the mixture passes the jell sheeting test. Stir the mixture constantly in order to prevent the bottom from burning.

Remove the mixture, skim off the red foam and pour the jelly into hot sterilized jelly jars. Seal while hot.

Blue Barberry Jelly

Use the same recipe as for Red Barberry. The jelly will have a lovely light blue color when finished.

Barberry Jam

    3 lbs. of ripe fruit
    2 cups of cold water
    1 cup of granulated sugar per cup of juice pulp

Place 3 lbs. of fully ripened and cleaned barberries into a saucepan and add 2 cups of water. Cook the mixture slowly over a moderate heat until the fruit softens. When thoroughly cooked, remove from the heat and pass the mixture through a fine sieve or strainer. This will remove the skins and seeds.

Measure the juicy pulp mixture, place into a saucepan and add 1 cup of granulated sugar for each cup of pulp. Mix well, bring to a boil, and hold there for 15 minutes, stirring constantly. Remove the foam and pour into hot sterile jelly jars. Seal while hot.

Barberry Sauce

    2 cups of cold water
    Grated rind of 1 orange
    2 cups of granulated sugar
    4 cups of ripe barberries

Place 2 cups of cold water, the fresh grated orange rind and 2 cups of granulated sugar into a saucepan. Mix well and cook over a moderate heat for 5 minutes. Add 4 cups of washed and stemmed barberries. Cook until berries begin to pop, about 5 minutes. When all berries have popped, place the sauce in a bowl and chill in a refrigerator. Serve chilled. This sauce has high concentrations of natural pectin and can be poured into a desired mold before chilling.

Pickled Barberry Relish

    1 pint of ripe fruit
    2 cups of granulated sugar
    4 cups of cider vinegar
    ½ teaspoon of ground allspice
    1 teaspoon of whole cloves
    1 stick of cinnamon

Wash and stem 1 pint of fully ripened barberries. Place into a deep saucepan, add 2 cups of granulated sugar and 4 cups of cider vinegar. Next add ½ teaspoon of ground allspice, 1 teaspoon of whole cloves and 1 stick of cinnamon. Bring to a boil and hold there until the fruits lose their color. Remove from the heat and allow to cool. Strain the mixture and pour into hot sterile pint jars and seal.

Spiced Barberry Jam

    2 lbs. of ripe berries
    1½ lbs. of sugar
    ½ pint diluted cider vinegar
    1 teaspoon each of: allspice
                     whole cloves
    1 cinnamon stick

Wash and stem 2 pounds of red ripe barberries. Make up a sauce of 1½ lbs. of granulated sugar and ½ pint of diluted cider vinegar. Add a spice bag of 1 teaspoon each of allspice, whole cloves and 1 stick of cinnamon. Bring the mixture to a boil for 1 full minute, then remove from the heat and cool. Next add the berries, heat slowly and simmer until berries are soft.

Remove from the heat, cover and place into a refrigerator to cool. Allow the mixture to remain overnight.

Next day, remove the spice bag, and pour off the sauce.

24

Pack the barberries into hot, sterile jars. Heat the syrup just to the boiling point, pour the hot juice over the berries and seal. Allow the fruit mixture to age for 1 month.

Barberry Conserve

    2 juice oranges
    2 quarts of ripe fruit
    ¾ teaspoon of cinnamon
    3 tablespoons of lemon juice
    4 cups of granulated sugar

Slice 2 juice oranges into very thin sections, removing the seeds. Cook the slices in a little water until tender.

Clean and stem 2 quarts of ripened barberries. Crush the fruit with a potato masher. Strain the pulp and juice through a strainer or food mill to remove the seeds. Add the juicy pulp to the cooked oranges and mix well. Add ¾ teaspoon of cinnamon, 3 tablespoons of lemon juice and 4 cups of granulated sugar. Mix well, bring to a boil, then simmer over a low heat until the sauce thickens. Remove from the heat, pour into hot sterile jelly jars and seal.

Bearberry

BEARBERRY
(Arctostaphylos uva-ursi)

A small shrubby plant that is usually found sprawling over the surface of the ground. It is highly branched with a height of 1–2 feet, depending on locale. The leaves are evergreen, smooth and somewhat leathery. The smaller twigs are generally covered with a fine hairy fuzz.

The small white flowers yield a red berry; smooth, somewhat mealy and bland tasting. Tannins present in some of the berries account for an acrid taste. Cooking destroys the tannins and improves the flavor. The berries appear on the vine in late summer or early fall. They may remain on the vine throughout the cold winter months. They become dried and more pulpy the longer they remain on the vine and therefore they should be harvested before any severe frost occurs. These small bushes usually bear a goodly supply of berries.

This plant ranges from the Arctic south to Pennsylvania. It thrives in open areas, especially in rock outcrops and mountain tops. The Alpine Bearberry *(A. alpinia)* is found in the Alaskan mountain ranges and it bears a blue-black berry.

Bearberry Jelly

> 2 quarts of berries
> 1 cup of granulated sugar per cup of juice
> 1 tablespoon lemon juice
> 3 ounces of liquid pectin

Select about 2 quarts of fully ripened berries, wash and stem. Place into a saucepan and cook until the fruit pops and the juice flows freely. Remove from the heat and squeeze through a jelly bag.

Measure the juice, place into a deep saucepan, add 1 cup of granulated sugar per cup of juice. Add 1 tablespoon of lemon juice, and mix thoroughly. Place the mixture over a high heat and boil until sugar dissolves. Stir constantly. Add 3 ounces of liquid pectin and keep the mixture at a hard boil for 1 full minute.

Skim off the beautiful deep red colored foam, pour into hot, sterile jelly jars and seal.

Bearberry Jam

2 quarts of fruit
1 cup of granulated sugar per cup of sauce
3 ounces of pectin

Place 2 quarts of washed, ripened fruit into a deep saucepan and cook over a moderate heat for 5 minutes. Remove from the heat and hand mash the fruit with a potato masher. Then force the mess through a strainer or a food mill in order to remove the seeds. Use as much of the juice and pulp as possible.

Measure the juice and pulp into a saucepan. Add 1 cup of granulated sugar to each cup of sauce. Mix well, bring to a boil for 1 minute, stirring the mixture constantly. Add 3 ounces of liquid pectin. Mix well. Boil for 1 minute. Pour into hot sterile jelly jars and seal.

Bearberry Paste

Collect, wash and stem 2 quarts of fresh bearberries. Place into a deep saucepan, add a little water and cook until the berries pop and the juice flows. Remove and pour through a sieve or food mill, extracting the seeds. Place the juicy pulp in a large bowl and cover, allowing the mixture to set for 24 hours.

Measure the juicy pulp, place in a deep saucepan, add 1 cup of granulated sugar for each cup of pureé. Mix well and boil for 10 minutes, stirring constantly. Pour into hot sterile jars and seal.

Spicy Bearberry Paste

Prepare the fruit exactly as you would in making bearberry paste. After you have placed the juicy pulp into a large bowl add the following ingredients: 1 crushed stick of cinnamon, 1 tablespoon of whole cloves and 1 teaspoon of allspice. Mix into the juicy pulp and allow to sit for 24 hours.

Strain the mixture, removing the whole spice particles and follow the remaining portion of the bearberry paste recipe.

Blackberries

BLACKBERRY

(Rubus sp.)

The species of blackberries are numerous and tasty. Blackberries range throughout most of North America. Creeping Blackberry *(R. procumbens)* and High Bush Blackberries *(R. allegheniensis)* are two of the more common species. Thimbleberries *(R. villosus)* can be found growing from New England west to Michigan and south to Florida.

The High Bush Blackberry is a tall plant (as depicted in the drawing), growing 3–7 feet in height. The canes contain an abundance of large thorns and the older canes have thorns large enough to penetrate heavy clothing.

The fruit is conical in shape, containing numerous small drupelets. The berries are pleasant to the taste, yet a little tart. When using the fruit as a cooked fruit it is wise to remove the central pithy substance unless the cooking time is such that it will cook away. Barely ripe blackberries, red in color, are high in natural pectins and jell very well. Fully ripened fruit are ideal for flavor but do not jelly very well as the pectin is greatly reduced.

The leaves are compound, with 3–5 leaflets, the terminal leaflet being the largest. The undersides are somewhat fuzzy and the margins are small toothed.

Blackberry Jelly (Quick Method)

> 2 quarts of ripe fruit
> 2½ cups of granulated sugar
>   juice of 1 lemon
> 3 ounces of liquid pectin

Clean and stem 2 quarts of fully ripened blackberries. Place the berries into a deep saucepan and crush or place through a foodmill. Once the fruit is completely crushed, place the mess into a jelly bag or cheese cloth and squeeze out just the juice. Measure out 2½ cups of the fine juice and place into a deep saucepan.

Now add 2½ cups of granulated sugar and mix well. Allow to stand for 10 minutes.

Mix 3 ounces of liquid pectin and the juice of 1 lemon in a separate bowl, then add to the blackberry juice. Stir for 3 minutes. Then add the concoction to hot sterile jelly jars and cover. The jelly should sit at room temperature for 24 hours, then store in a freezer for 4 weeks. Thaw and use when needed.

Blackberry Jelly (Cooked)

> 2½ quarts of blackberries
> Juice of 2 lemons
> 5 cups of granulated sugar
> 3 ounces of pectin

Clean and wash 2½ quarts of fully ripened fruit. Place in a container and crush completely, or use a food mill of some type. Next, heat the mixture until the juice approaches boiling. Now allow the juice to simmer over a low heat for 10 minutes.

Remove from the heat and pour the mixture into a jelly bag or cheese cloth. Recover 3 cups of the juice and place into a deep saucepan. Add the juice of 2 lemons or ¼ cup of reconstituted lemon juice. Stir well. Add 5 cups of granulated sugar and mix well. Next place the mixture over a high heat and bring to a boil. Stir constantly. Add 3 ounces of liquid pectin and bring to a boil for 1 full minute, stirring constantly.

Remove from the heat, skim off the colorful foam (eat if you wish—it tastes just super!) and pour the juice into hot sterile jelly glasses. Once jelled, it can be used immediately.

Blackberry-Apple Jelly

> 3 cups of apple juice
> 3 cups of blackberry juice
> 3-5 tablespoons of lemon juice
> 7 cups of granulated sugar

Barely ripened apples contain high concentrations of natural pectin, whereas fully ripened blackberries contain little natural pectin. By blending the juice of these two fruits, you can produce a delightful natural jelly.

To prepare the apples, select any type of cooking or eating apple that is less than 25% ripe. Wash well to remove any grime or sprays. Slice the apples into quarters, remove the blossoms and stem. Place into a deep saucepan, cores, skin and all. Add just enough cold water to cover the sections, cover and bring to a boil. Use enough apples to produce 3 cups of apple juice. (Add more if you wish to produce a cup of refreshing drink while you work.) Reduce the heat and simmer for about 15 minutes.

Remove from the heat and crush the apple sections. Place back on the heat and cook for 5 minutes. Once completely cooked, place the mess into a jelly bag and allow to drip into a bowl, do not squeeze. Recover 3 cups of apple juice.

To prepare the blackberries, clean and wash while the apples simmer. Place in a large enough container and crush. Crush enough fruit to produce 3 cups of juice. Heat the mess until the juice approaches boiling point. Allow the juice to simmer over a low heat for 10 minutes. Remove and pour through a jelly bag, obtaining as much as you can. Collect 3 full cups of juice.

Now blend 3 cups of apple juice and 3 cups of blackberry juice together in a deep saucepan. Cook for 5 minutes. Add 7 cups of granulated sugar and 3–5 tablespoons of lemon juice, if the fruit juice is not tart enough. Next, allow the mixture to boil for 1 full minute, then remove from the heat. Skim off the colorful foam and pour the juice into hot, sterile jelly glasses.

Blackberry Jam

    2 quarts of blackberries
    7 cups of granulated sugar
    3 ounces of pectin

Completely crush about 2 quarts of fully ripened berries and remove about ½ the pulp and seeds, using a strainer. Recover 4 cups of the juicy pulp and place into a deep saucepan. Add 7 cups of granulated sugar and mix well. Bring to a boil for 1 full minute.

Add 3 ounces of liquid pectin and mix thoroughly. Bring to a boil, hold for 1 full minute. Stir constantly. Skim off the colorful foam and allow to cool for 3–5 minutes. Pour into hot, sterile jelly jars and seal.

Blackberry-Honey Jam

Follow the recipe for blackberry jam as indicated. Instead of using granulated sugar, use 4 cups of honey. The color of the jam will not be as dark, rather much lighter, but very pleasing. You may vary the amount of honey, depending on your taste for sweets. You may also want to add a stick of cinnamon, ground to a fine powder, just to add a little touch to the flavor.

Blackberry Juice

Add fresh blackberries to a blender and crush until a fine soup is produced. Keep adding fruit until 2 quarts of juice is obtained. Pour the juice through a few layers of cheesecloth, just to remove the pulp and seeds.

Next add 2 cups of lemon juice and—voilá—you have an excellent summer beverage. Serve chilled for best flavor. This fine drink can also be frozen and used during the winter months to do away with those cold winter blahs.

Blackberry Wine

Select 4 lbs. of fully ripened berries, place into a very large saucepan, add 6 pints of water. Bring to a gentle boil and hold there for 15 minutes. Remove the juice with a press or jelly bag.

To each quart of juice add 2 cups of granulated sugar, and mix thoroughly. Next pour the sweetened juice into 1 gallon containers. Large crocks are preferred, but gallon (glass) jugs will do. Add a cake of live yeast and cover with cotton plugs.

Allow to stand for one week. Sterilize more gallon jugs and pour off the fermented juice into these sterile jugs. Cap with wads of sterile cotton, this will keep out wild yeast and dirt.

Store in a cool, dark place until the brew clears and there is no evidence of further fermentation. All bubbling has ceased. Once all fermentation has ceased, carefully decant or pour off the top portion of the brew, leaving the cloudy residue behind. Pour the clarified liquid into sterile quart wine bottles and cap or cork. Allow to stand in order to age, for at least 3–5 months.

33

Black Gum

BLACK GUM
(Nyssa sylvatica)

A small tree of 20–30 feet, Black Gum can be found throughout most of the mountainous areas of eastern United States. It ranges from Maine south to Florida and west to Michigan and Texas. It thrives in wet areas.

The leaves have a dark olive green color and turn a spectacular maroon color in the fall. The berry-like fruit is ovoid, about ½ inch long and black with a purple sheen. Commonly found in pairs, the fruit usually ripens in early September. It is edible raw, but cooking enhances the flavor. Depending on the birds, the fruit can be found still on the trees throughout the winter months.

Delightful colored and flavored jellies have been made for many years from these colorful fruits. They can be cooked into a beautiful blue-colored sauce that is used to enhance the flavor of meat.

The trunk of the tree can also be tapped, much in the same manner of the Sugar Maple *(Acer saccharum)*. The sap flows rather abundantly in the early spring. The sap has a rather tart taste, but when allowed to dry, it can be used as a gum for chewing.

Black Gum Jelly

> 2 quarts of berries
> ½ cup of water
> 1 cup of sugar per cup of juice
> 3 ounces of liquid pectin

Collect 2 quarts of black gum berries. These ½ inch long berries will have a blue-black color when fully ripe. Discard overripe fruit. Wash and stem, then place in a deep saucepan. Add ½ cup of cold water and bring to a boil. Reduce the heat and continue to cook until the fruit bursts and the juice runs free.

Next pour the cooked mixture through a jelly bag or cheese cloth. Measure the juice, place into a deep saucepan, add 1 cup of granulated sugar to each cup of juice. Bring to a boil and stir constantly until the sugar has dissolved. Add 3 ounces of liquid pectin, stir and boil hard for 1 full minute. Stir constantly to prevent burning. Skim off the colorful blue foam and pour the hot liquid into sterile jelly jars and seal.

Spicy Black Gum Jelly

2 quarts of berries
½ cup of water
1 cup of sugar per cup of juice
3 ounces of liquid pectin
1 stick of cinnamon
3 tablespoons of whole cloves
1 teaspoon of allspice

Use the same procedures as in the making of black gum jelly, add the above spices. After you measure out the juice, add the above spices to the juice and simmer for 10 minutes. Remove the spices; then add 1 cup of granulated sugar to each cup of juice. Bring to a boil and follow the rest of the recipe.

Black Gum Jam

2 quarts of berries
½ cup of water
1 cup of sugar per cup of juice
3 ounces of liquid pectin

Clean 2 quarts of black gum fruit, place the berries into a deep saucepan and cook until soft and the juice flows. With a hand masher, crush the fruit completely. Run through a sieve or food mill removing the skins and seeds.

Measure the juicy pulp and place into a deep saucepan. Add 1 cup of granulated sugar for each cup of juicy pulp and mix thoroughly. Bring to a boil and hold for 1 minute. Stir constantly. Add 3 ounces of liquid pectin and boil for 1 full minute.

Remove the colorful foam and pour into hot sterile jelly jars and seal.

Haw, Black

BLACK HAW
(Viburnum prunifolium)

An erect, widely spreading shrub, Black Haw will attain heights to 20 feet or more. It can be found growing in dry soils and has a range from New England south to Georgia. Southern Black Haw *(V. rufidulum)* is a similar species. It has a growth range from Virginia south to Florida and west to Texas.

The leaves are broad, ovate in shape and deep green, with sharp-toothed margins. The flowers are white and in large clusters of 2–5 inches across. These large flower clusters yield clusters of ovoid berries that are dark blue in color. These succulent berries are quite sweet and therefore make excellent jellies and jams. The fruit is generally found ripened from late August to late September, if the birds do not eat them first. The berries do lack in natural pectin.

Black Haw Jelly

> 1 quart of fruit
> 1 cup of sugar per cup of juice
> 3 ounces of pectin

Wash and stem 1 quart of fully ripened black haw fruit. Place the fruit into a deep saucepan, with a little water and bring to a boil. Reduce the heat and cook the fruit until the berries pop. Remove from the heat and run the mixture through a food mill or strainer. Pass the resulting juice through a jelly bag. Do not squeeze.

Measure the juice, place into a deep saucepan, add 1 cup of granulated sugar to each cup of juice. Bring to a boil and stir constantly until the sugar has dissolved. Now add 3 ounces of liquid pectin, boil hard for 1 full minute, skim off the foam and pour the jelly into hot, sterile jelly jars.

Spicy Black Haw Jelly

> 1 quart of fruit
> 1 cup of water
> 1 cup of sugar per cup of juice
> 1 stick of cinnamon
> 1 tablespoon of whole cloves
> 1 teaspoon of ground allspice

Wash and stem 1 quart of fully ripened fruit. Place the fruit into a deep saucepan and add 1 cup of water. Add the spices in a spice bag and cook the mixture until the fruit pops and the juice runs freely. Remove the spice bag and run the mixture through a jelly bag. Do not squeeze.

Measure the juice, place into a deep saucepan, add 1 cup of sugar to each cup of juice. Mix well and bring to a boil. Add 3 ounces of liquid pectin, boil hard for 1 minute, then skim off the foam. Pour the hot sauce into hot, sterile jelly jars and seal.

Black Haw Jam

    1 quart of fruit
    1 cup of sugar per cup of juice
    ½ cup of water
    3 ounces of pectin

Wash and stem 1 quart of fully ripened black haws. Place the fruit into a deep saucepan, add ½ cup of water, and cook until fruit pops. With a hand masher crush the fruit completely. Run the mess through a food mill or strainer. This will remove the skins and seeds.

Measure the juicy pulp and place into a deep saucepan. Add 1 cup of granulated sugar for each cup of sauce. Bring to a boil, then add 3 ounces of liquid pectin. Boil and stir for 1 full minute. Remove from heat and skim off the colorful blue foam. Pour into hot, sterile jelly jars and seal.

Spiced Black Haws

    1 quart of berries
    ¼ cup of white vinegar
    1½ cups of sugar
        Spices: 1 stick of cinnamon
                   4–6 whole cloves
                   1 teaspoon of allspice

Wash and stem 1 quart of fully ripened berries and place them in a deep saucepan. Make up a spice bag of, 1 stick of cinnamon, 4–6 whole cloves and 1 teaspoon of allspice. Add ¼ cup of white or clear vinegar and 1½ cups of granulated sugar. Mix thoroughly. Add the spice bag and simmer the mixture over a low heat until mixture thickens. Stir occasionally.

Remove the spice bag and allow to sit a few minutes. This will allow the fruit to settle. Spoon the fruit mixture into hot, sterile jars. Seal immediately. Allow 1 month or more before serving.

Black Haw Conserve

2 juice oranges
1½ quarts of black haws
¾ teaspoon of ground cinnamon
3 tablespoons of lemon juice
3 cups granulated sugar

Slice 2 juice oranges into very thin sections, removing the seeds. Cook the orange slices in a little water until tender.

Clean and stem about 1½ quarts of black haw fruit. Crush the fruit in a pan with a hand masher. (Do not use a blender as it will pulverize the seeds.) Strain the pulpy mess through a strainer or a food mill, removing the seeds. Add the juicy pulp to the cooked oranges and mix well.

Add ¾ teaspoon of ground cinnamon, 3 tablespoons of lemon juice, and 3 cups of granulated sugar. Mix thoroughly and simmer over a low heat until sauce thickens. Allow to cool a few minutes then spoon the conserve into hot, sterile jars and seal.

Black Haw Relish

2 quarts of black haw fruit
3 cups of cider vinegar
1 cup of sugar
1 tablespoon of ground allspice
1 tablespoon of ground cinnamon
½ teaspoon of cayenne pepper
6 whole cloves

Wash and stem 2 quarts of fully ripened black haw berries. Place into a deep saucepan, add 3 cups of cider vinegar and cook until the fruit softens. Remove from the heat and run the mixture through a strainer to remove the seeds.

Put the juicy pulp and the skins of the fruit into a deep saucepan. Add 1 cup of granulated sugar, add the spices and mix thoroughly. Simmer over a low heat until the mix thickens. Stir occassionally. Pour the mix into hot, sterile jars and seal. This formula should yield about 3 pints of relish.

Black Haw Juice

Add 2 quarts of fully ripened black haw fruit to a deep saucepan. Cook for a period of 5–6 minutes, then crush the fruit completely. Add 1 cup of water and simmer for 5 minutes.

Remove the juicy pulp, run through a few layers of cheese cloth. Collect the juice, add 1 cup of lemon juice and mix thoroughly. Serve chilled, can also be frozen as iced black haw.

Black Haw Wine

Crush 3½ pounds of fully ripened black haw fruit. Remove the seeds and skins by strainer or food mill. Place the juicy pulp into a deep pan. Add 1 quart of cooled sterile water. Mix well with the juicy pulp. Allow the mix to set for 1 hour, covered.

Add 1 lb. of granulated sugar to 1½ quarts of water and bring to a boil for 2 minutes. Place the sugar mixture into a large ceramic crock. Add the fruit juice and 1 cake of Baker's yeast or any all purpose wine yeast. Cover the crock and allow the pulp to ferment for 7 days.

Then strain the mixture through a jelly bag and squeeze completely. Recover at least 1 gallon of strained fermented juice. Boil 1 lb. of granulated sugar in 1 quart of water. Cool and add to the mixture. Mix thoroughly, then pour it off into a sterile gallon jug and stopper loosely with sterile cotton wool.

Place the jug in a warm dark place, about 70° F. for about 8–10 days. Carefully decant into quart bottles and tightly stopper. Cork stoppers are best. Allow a few months to season and serve chilled.

Blueberries

BLUEBERRY
(Vaccinium sp.)

There are some 20 or more species of Vaccinium found scattered throughout most of Canada and the United States. They can be found on mountain tops of 2,000 feet and in lowland bogs.

The Highbush Blueberry *(V. corymbosum)* grows as a shrub to a height of 10 feet or more. The Lowbush Blueberry *(V. pennsylvanicum)* and the Late Lowbush Blueberry *(V. vacitlans)* usually attain heights of 1–2 feet and yield ripe fruit as soon as late June in warmer climates, and later in cooler climates. The Lowbush Blueberry grows best in open, exposed areas and in higher elevations.

The Blueberry is certainly one of the finest, if not the finest, wild fruit that grows in the wild. The small wild Blueberry has more color and taste than does the much larger cultivated varieties, which are not as sweet. To enhance their flavor, use at least 50% red (partially ripe) berries.

The leaves are small: 2–3 inches long, 1½ inches wide, bright green, lighter green undersides, with entire margins. The leaves alternate on the stems. The flowers appear at about the same time the leaves do. They are borne in clusters and yield fruit in small but heavy clusters.

There is always some confusion as to Blueberries and Huckleberries. To most individuals there appears to be no difference; to the Botanist there are fine differences. Whatever the slight differences may be, they are both excellent food fare and can be used for pies, jellies, jams, tarts and just plain eating out of hand.

Blueberry Jelly (Waterless)

> 6 cups of blueberries
> 9 cups of sugar
> 3 ounces of pectin

Blueberry jelly is quite expensive to make as well as to buy, if you can find it. Select berries that are slightly underripe, or use at least 50% of the berries red and the rest fully ripe. This will add a superlative flavor to your jelly.

43

Wash and clean 6 cups of blueberries, either crush with a masher or use a blender on slow speed. Once mashed, add to a deep saucepan and gently cook for 10 minutes or until the juice rolls. Then strain the juice through a jelly bag. Add 9 cups of granulated sugar.

Bring the blueberry mix to a full boil for 1 minute, stir constantly to prevent bottom burn. Next add 3 ounces of liquid pectin. Hold at a boil for 1 minute and stir constantly.

Skim off the colorful and tasty foam (try it) and pour the sauce into hot, sterile jelly jars and seal.

Blueberry Jelly (Cooked)

9 cups of blueberries
¾ cup of sugar per cup of juice
½ cup of water
3 ounces of liquid pectin

Wash and clean 9 cups of 50% red and 50% ripe berries. Place into a deep saucepan and crush. Add ½ cup of water. Place the mixture over a medium heat and simmer for about 5 minutes. Remove and allow the mix to drip through a jelly bag. Recover the juice and measure.

Now add ¾ of a cup of granulated sugar to each cup of juice and mix well in a deep saucepan.

Bring the mixture to a boil. Add 3 ounces of liquid pectin and hold at a boil for 1 full minute. Stir constantly. Drain off the colorful foam and pour the sauce into hot, sterile jelly jars and seal.

Blueberry-Mint Jelly

9 cups of berries
¾ cup of fresh mint leaves
¾ cup of sugar per cup of juice
3 ounces of liquid pectin
1½ cups of water

Wash and clean 9 cups of ripe berries. Crush in a deep saucepan or in a blender. Place in a deep saucepan and add ½ cup of mint infusion.

To make the mint infusion, take ¾ cup of crushed fresh mint leaves. Place in a separate saucepan and add 1½ cups of water and bring to a boil. Remove from the heat, cover and allow to stand for 10 minutes. Then strain the mint solution through layered cheese cloth. Measure out ½ cup of the infusion. (Drink the rest for a real treat!)

Place the mint-berry mixture over a moderate heat and simmer for 5 minutes. Remove, then strain the mixture through a jelly bag. Measure the juice and add ¾ cup of granulated sugar to each cup of juice. Mix well and bring to a boil. Add 3 ounces of liquid pectin, stir constantly for 1 full minute.

Skim off the sweet flavored foam, pour into hot, sterile jelly jars and seal.

Blueberry-Sour Cherry Jelly

    1 quart fully ripe berries
    2 pounds of sour cherries
    ½ cup of water
    4½ cups of sugar
    3 ounces of pectin

Thoroughly crush the blueberries in a deep saucepan or blender. Then add either pitted or un-pitted sour cherries to a separate saucepan and mash. (Do not attempt to mash the cherries with pits in a blender.) Now add the two mashed fruits into a deep saucepan, add ½ cup of water. Place over the heat and bring to a boil. Allow to simmer for 10 minutes, keeping the pan covered.

Remove from the heat and place in a jelly bag and allow the juices to flow freely. Recover the juices and combine with 4½ cups of granulated sugar in a deep saucepan, mix well until the sugar is dissolved. Bring to a boil, add 3 ounces of liquid pectin and hold at a boil for 1 full minute. Stir constantly, do not burn. Skim off the tasty foam, pour into hot, sterile jelly jars and seal.

Blueberry Jam

    9 cups of ripe berries
    ½ cup of water
    ¾ cup of sugar per cup of sauce

Wash and stem 9 cups of fully ripened berries. Crush in a deep saucepan, add ½ cup of water and cook over a moderate heat for 5 minutes. Measure the sauce and add ¾ cup of granulated sugar to each cup of sauce. Mix thoroughly and bring to a boil. Add 3 ounces of liquid pectin and hold at a boil for 1 full minute. Skim off the colorful foam, pour into hot, sterile jelly jars and seal.

Blueberry-Maple Syrup Sauce

4 cups of ripe berries
¾ cup of maple syrup

Wash and stem 4 cups of fully ripened berries. Crush the berries in a deep saucepan. Cook over a moderate heat for 5 minutes. Remove from the heat, add ¾ cup of maple syrup. Mix thoroughly. Place over a moderate heat until thoroughly mixed. Remove from the heat and serve while hot. Terrific when used as a topping for ice cream.

The same effect can be achieved if you use blueberry jam in place of the fresh berries.

Buffalo Berry

BUFFALO BERRY
(Shepherdia argentea)

A shrub or small tree, Buffalo Berry is somewhat thorny and will attain heights of 10–30 feet. It is a native shrub of North America and is often used as an ornamental species. As an ornamental, the name Silverleaf is quite common. It grows in the wild with a range from Alaska south to California and east to Massachusetts, south to the Carolinas.

The shrub has a scraggy appearance, light gray twigs with thorns and bears simple leaves. They are narrow, oblong, rounded at the tip, silvery-colored on both surfaces and have entire margins. The flowers appear in April and yield a dull red ovid fruit about ¼ inches long. The fruit contains a single seed. The fruit is also quite acidic but edible with a taste similar to that of the wild red currant.

This shrub is a very prolific producer with branches laden with fruit. Much of the fruit remains on the shrub throughout the cold winter months. Cooking greatly improves the acid taste.

Buffalo Berry Jelly

> 1 quart ripe berries
> ½ cup cold water
> 1½ cups of sugar per cup of juice
> 3 ounces of liquid pectin

Wash and stem 1 quart of fully ripened berries, place into a deep saucepan, add ½ cup of cold water and bring to a boil. Simmer for 10 minutes. Crush with a potato masher and simmer again for 5 minutes. Run the sauce through a food mill, then through a jelly bag. Measure the fruit juice, add 1½ cups of granulated sugar to each cup of juice. Mix well and bring to a boil. Add 3 ounces of liquid pectin and bring to a boil for 1 full minute. Stir constantly. Skim off the colorful foam, pour the sauce into hot, sterile jelly jars and seal.

Buffalo Berry Conserve

4 cups of ripe berries
1½ cups of water
¼ pound chopped seedless raisins
½ cup chopped nut meats
1 chopped orange
8 cups sugar

Wash and clean 4 cups of fully ripened berries. Add to a deep saucepan with 1½ cups of water. Cook until the berries have softened. Stir occasionally. Add ¼ pound of chopped seedless raisins, ½ cup of chopped nut meats (walnuts), 1 chopped orange and 8 cups of granulated sugar. Mix well and stir constantly. Cook the mixture 20–30 minutes. Then skim off the foam, spoon into hot, sterile jelly jars and seal.

Buffalo Berry Spicy Sauce

4 cups of berries
Grated rind of 1 orange
2 cups of water
2 cups of sugar
¼ teaspoon of ground cinnamon
Pinch of ground cloves

Combine the grated rind of a fresh orange, 2 cups of water and 2 cups of granulated sugar in a saucepan. Mix and cook over a moderate heat for 10 minutes. Add 4 cups of cleaned berries. Cook until the berries pop. Now add ¼ teaspoon of ground cinnamon, a pinch of ground cloves and cook for 5 minutes. Stir frequently.

Spoon the mixture into a bowl and place into the refrigerator to chill. Serve chilled. This is a delightful red colored, spicy sauce and is best served with meat as a flavoring.

Canada Mayflower

CANADA MAYFLOWER

(Mainanthemum canadense)

This little member of the Lily family grows in great abundance in pine wood areas. A low ground plant, it grows to a height of 5—7 inches and in somewhat large, scattered clumps. The single erect stem arises from a slender rootstock. The stem bears 1—3 leaves on a zig-zag stem. This small plant ranges from southern Canada south to the Carolinas and west to Iowa.

The flowers are borne in a terminal cluster. They are fragile, white and small. They yield greenish-white berries that turn pink, then bright ruby red. The berries appear in late June and ripen in August. Some varieties produce pink-red, speckled fruit. The entire plant is edible.

The ripened berries are tart, acidic, fleshy and have the flavor of cranberries. The fruit contains high concentrations of vitamins A and C.

Canada Mayflower Jelly

> 1 quart of berries
> 1 cup sugar per cup of juice
> 3 ounces pectin

Gather 1 heaping quart of fully ripened berries. Do not use berries that are puckered or dehydrated. Wash and stem. Place into a saucepan, add a little water, cover and cook over a moderate heat until fruit pops. Remove from the heat and force through a jelly bag.

Measure the juice and add 1 cup of granulated sugar to each cup of juice. These berries have a tart taste and therefore you may want to vary the amount of sugar, according to your own taste.

Bring to a boil, add 3 ounces of liquid pectin and boil for 1 full minute. Stir constantly. Skim off the colorful foam, pour into hot, sterile jelly jars and seal.

Canada Mayflower Spice Jelly

    4 cups of ripe fruit
    ⅓ cup of water
    ¾ cup of vinegar
    4 cups of sugar
    1 tablespoon of ground cinnamon
    ½ tablespoon of ground allspice
    4 whole cloves
    3 ounces of pectin

Wash and stem 4 cups of fully ripened berries, discarding dried fruit. Place in a deep saucepan, add ⅓ cup of water, ¾ cup of vinegar, 1 tablespoon of ground cinnamon, ½ tablespoon of ground allspice, 4 whole cloves and 4 cups of granulated sugar. Mix thoroughly, place over a low heat and simmer for 30 minutes. Stir occasionally to prevent bottom burn.

Remove from the heat, force through a food mill then through a jelly bag. Recover the juice. Place the mixture into a deep saucepan, bring to a boil. Add 3 ounces of liquid pectin and hold at a hard boil for 1 full minute. Remove from the heat, skim off the foam, pour into hot, sterile jelly jars and seal.

Canada Mayflower-Crab Apple Jelly

    1 quart of ripe berries
    6—8 medium crab apples
    1 cup of sugar per cup of juice

Select only fully ripened fruit, discarding dehydrated berries. Wash and stem 1 full quart of berries, add them to a saucepan and cook in a small amount of water until berries pop and the juice runs free.

Wash and stem 6—8 medium sized crab apples. Remove the flower sections and core. Cut the fruit into eighths. Cook in a saucepan with 2 tablespoons of water for 20—30 minutes. Crush with a food masher. Combine both fruits in a food mill, extract the watery pulp and run through a jelly bag. Do not squeeze the bag.

Measure the pulp and add 1 cup of granulated sugar to each cup of juice. Mix thoroughly in a deep saucepan. Bring the mixture to a boil for 2 full minutes. Skim off the foam; pour into hot, sterile jelly jars and seal.

The color of the jelly may blanch somewhat, this can be corrected by adding a few peels of bright colored red crab apples. This will add extra pigment to the sauce and brighten it considerably.

Canada Mayflower Spicy Sauce

1 teaspoon grated orange rind
2 cups of ripe fruit
1 cup granulated sugar
½ teaspoon allspice
2 whole cloves
1 cup of water

Add 1 cup of granulated sugar and 1 cup of water to a saucepan. Mix and bring to a boil for 5 minutes.

Wash and stem 2 cups of berries, place in a deep saucepan with a little water and boil for 2 minutes. Remove from the heat and force the cooked fruit through a food mill. Obtain as much of the juicy pulp as possible.

Combine the juicy pulp and syrup in a deep saucepan. Add the spices and mix thoroughly. Simmer the mix until thick. This should take from 5–10 minutes. Add the grated orange rind. Cook for 1 minute, then serve. It has the special flavor of cranberries and can be used as an excellent garnish for meats.

Carrion Flower

CARRION FLOWER
(Smilax herbacea)

This unusual member of the Lily family produces a bluish-black berry, that has a very pleasant flavor. Greenish-white flower clusters appear in June and have a rather noxious scent, that of decaying flesh (carrion); hence its name. This unpleasant odor causes many people to shy from this unusual plant as a food source.

A climbing vine, it will attain heights of 10—15 feet. It can usually be found growing in meadows, thickets, over any type of shrub that thrives in open areas. It has a growth range from New Brunswick south to Georgia and west to the Rocky Mountains.

The fruit clusters appear in mid-July and ripen during late August. These berry clusters are many, and several pounds of fruit may be taken from just a single 20 foot vine. The fruit can be eaten raw.

The dark blue-black color makes a very impressive colored jelly or sauce. The amount of pectin in the fruit is sufficient to set up the cooked fruit without additional pectin. The fruit sauce is excellent to baste wild meats, and it adds zest and flavor.

Carrion Flower Jelly

2 quarts of berries
½ cup of sugar per cup of juice

Select, wash, and stem 2 quarts of fully ripened berries. They will be a little pulpy, but quite useable. Place into a saucepan with a little water and cook over a moderate heat until fruit softens. Crush the fruit with a food masher and let cook for 5 minutes. Stir occasionally.

Remove from the heat and squeeze through a jelly bag. Recover the juice and measure. Add ½ cup of granulated sugar to each cup of juice. Place the mix over a high heat and boil until sugar dissolves. Cook the mix until a positive jelly "sheet" test results. Skim off the blue foam, pour into hot, sterile jelly jars and seal.

Carrion Flower Spice Jelly

    4 cups of berries
    ½ cup of water
    ¾ cup of cider vinegar
    1 tablespoon of ground cinnamon
    1 teaspoon of ground allspice
    6 whole cloves
    4 cups of sugar
    3 ounces of pectin

Wash and stem 4 cups of fully ripened berries. Place them into a deep saucepan with ½ cup of water, ¾ cup of cider vinegar, 1 tablespoon of ground cinnamon, 1 teaspoon of ground allspice, 6 whole cloves and 4 cups of granulated sugar. Mix the ingredients.

Place the mix over a low heat and cook for 30 minutes, stirring occasionally. Pour the sauce through a fine sieve, place into a deep saucepan, add 3 ounces of liquid pectin, bring to a boil for 1 full minute. Skim off the foam, pour the sauce into hot, sterile jelly jars and seal.

Carrion Flower Purée

Collect whatever amount of fruit you desire. Place into a deep saucepan, add a little water and cook until fruit softens. With carrion flower berries you may use dried berries as they will re-hydrate.

Mash the fruit and strain, removing the seeds. Then strain the sauce through a jelly bag. Use the juice for jelly, but save the pulp for a delightful purée. Allow the pulp to sit overnight in a cool place, covered.

The following day, remove the purée, add 1 cup of granulated sugar to each cup of pulp. Place into a saucepan, mix and bring to a boil. Cook at a boil for 8–10 minutes, stirring constantly. Remove from the heat and serve or can as you would jelly.

Cherry, Wild Black

CHERRY, WILD BLACK
(Prunus sp.)

There are several species of Wild Cherry located throughout most of the United States and southern Canada. The more common ones include: Chokecherry *(P. virginiana)*, Pin Cherry *(P. pennsylvanica)*, Sand Cherry *(P. pumita)*, Sweet Cherry *(P. avium)*, Chicasaw Plum or Mountain Cherry *(P. angustifolia)* and the Black Cherry *(P. serotina)*. All have considerable merit as wild fruits. They may vary in abundance, size, color and certainly taste.

Many of the wild species are commonly used as ornamental species and so it is very easy to find such fruiting trees. They may simply be in someone's yard.

The fruit is usually available from August through September. They can be eaten raw from the trees or used in jellies or sauces. These particular wild fruits do not contain enough natural pectins; therefore additional pectin will be necessary.

When used as a food source the cherry has a caloric value of 65 per 4 ounces of fruit and 650 i.u. of vitamin A. It makes either a sweet or tart jelly, depending on the particular type of cherry.

Pin Cherry Jelly

12 cups of pin cherries
2 cups of water
7 cups of sugar
6 ounces of pectin

Clean 12 cups of pin cherries, place into a deep saucepan with 2 cups of water and cook over a low heat for 20–30 minutes or until all of the cherries have popped their skins.

Strain the juice through a jelly bag. Collect 3½ cups of juice, place into a deep saucepan, add 7 cups of granulated sugar, mix well and bring to a boil, stirring constantly. Add 6 ounces of liquid pectin. Hold at a boil for 1 full minute. Remove from the heat, skim off the foam, pour into hot, sterile jelly jars and seal.

Chokecherry Jelly

12 cups of chokecherries
3 cups of water
6½ ounces of sugar
6 ounces of pectin

Clean and stem 12 cups of fully ripened fruit, place into a saucepan, add 3 cups of water and bring to a boil. Lower the heat and simmer over a low heat for about 15 minutes or until the cherries pop their skins.

Strain the mixture through a jelly bag. Measure 3 full cups of the juice into a deep saucepan. Add 6½ cups of sugar and mix thoroughly. The sauce will be a little tart. Add more sugar if you like your jellies sweet.

Bring to a boil, add 6 ounces of liquid pectin and boil for 1 full minute. Remove from the heat, skim off the foam, pour into hot, sterile jelly jars and seal.

Cherry-Currant Jelly

12 cups of wild cherries
16 cups of ripe currants
¾ cup of water
7 cups of granulated sugar
3 ounces of pectin

Wash, stem and crush 12 cups of fully ripened wild cherries. Separately crush 12 cups of ripe currants. Red currants are preferred as they will enhance the color of the jelly.

Combine the fruit mixes in a deep saucepan, add ¾ cup of water, bring to a boil, then simmer over a low heat for about 10 minutes. This will release the juice from the pulp of the two fruits. Strain the mixture through a jelly bag.

Recover 4½ cups of juice. Add 7 cups of granulated sugar, bring to a boil and add 3 ounces of liquid pectin. Stir constantly and bring to a boil for 1 full minute. Skim off the colorful foam, pour the hot mixture into hot, sterile jelly jars and seal.

Wild Cherry-Crab Apple Jelly

12 cups of wild cherries
10 medium crab apples
7 cups of sugar
¾ cup of water

Wash and stem 10 medium sized crab apples, core and cut into eighths. Place into a saucepan with a little water and cook until the juice runs free.

Wash and stem 12 cups of wild cherries, place into a saucepan with ¾ cup of water. Cook until fruit pops. Remove from the heat and strain both fruit sauces through a jelly bag. Recover the juices, mix in a saucepan, add 7 cups of granulated sugar and mix thoroughly. Bring to a boil then simmer over a low heat about 10 minutes. Allow to cook until "sheeting" of the sauce is reached. Remove from the heat, skim off any foam, pour into hot, sterile jelly jars and seal.

Black Cherry Conserve

2 juice oranges
1 quart of wild cherries
¾ teaspoon of ground cinnamon
6 tablespoons of lemon juice
3½ cups sugar

Cut 2 juice oranges into thin slices, remove the seeds, place in a deep saucepan and cover with water. Cook until skins are tender.

Stem and clean 1 quart of wild cherries. Strain the wild cherries through a food mill. This will remove the pits. Add the juicy pulp to the cooked orange slices and mix. Next add the spices, lemon juice and sugar. Mix thoroughly and simmer over a low heat until thick. The mixture will appear somewhat clear when ready.

Remove from the heat; spoon the mixture into hot, sterile jelly jars and seal.

Wild Cherry Jam

3 lbs. of wild cherries
7 cups of sugar
3 ounces of pectin

Any of the wild cherries can be used to make a fine tasting jam, however, the amount of sugar required will vary according to the sweetness of the jam you desire.

Stem and clean 3 lbs. of wild cherries. Pit, chop or grind. You may also strain the fruit through a food mill. This will remove the pits. Collect 4 cups of the juicy pulp. Add 6 or 7 cups of granulated sugar and mix thoroughly. Bring to a boil, add 3 ounces of liquid pectin and hold at a hard boil for 1 full minute. Stir constantly.

Remove from the heat, skim off the colorful foam, pour the sauce into hot, sterile jelly jars and seal. The jam will take 20–30 minutes to set up.

Wild Cherry Sauce

> 4 cups of wild cherries
> ¼ cup of sugar
> 1 tablespoon of orange juice

Stew 4 cups of chokecherries or black cherries for about 20 minutes. Remove from the heat and strain. Separate the pulp from the juice. Use a jelly bag or a fine strainer, but remove the pits and skins.

Mix 1 cup of strained pulp, ⅓ cup of juice and ¼ cup of sugar. Simmer over a low heat for 10 minutes. Stir constantly to prevent burning.

Remove from the heat, add 1 tablespoon of fresh orange juice, mix and serve. This type of sauce can be used to baste wild meats or lamb to enhance their flavor. It can also be used as a topping for ice cream.

Choke Pears

CHOKE PEARS
(Pyrus communis)

The Pear was first brought to North America from Europe, but since then has escaped from cultivation to the wilds. A strange tree when in the wild, it may be 5—6 feet in circumference and 20 or more feet in height.

The branches are stubby, rough and somewhat scaly. They bear leaves that are entire or finely toothed, pointed tips, ovate and rounded at the base. The leaves and flowers arise from the terminus of the branch.

The flowers are small, an inch or so across and generally white in color. These small flowers yield a small 2 inch fruit that has the typical teardrop or pear shape. This particular fruit is not too agreeable to the palate, hence the name, Choke Pear. In most instances cooking greatly enhances the flavor. The fruit generally is ripe in late summer or early autumn, depending on climate and location.

This wild fruit can be found growing in non-competitive marginal areas such as thickets, old orchards, field edges and fence rows. It has a range from Maine south to Pennsylvania, and northern sections of Virginia and Tennessee.

Once located, it is evident the abundance of fruit is well worth the search. The fruit is hard and the solid flesh makes it highly desirable for pickling and relishes.

Pear Jam

> 3 lbs. of ripe fruit
> ½ the juice of 1 lemon
> 6 cups sugar
> 3 ounces pectin

Weigh out about 3 pounds of fully ripe fruit. Peel and core. Chop the fruit into small sections. Measure out 4 cups of chopped pears. Place in a deep saucepan and add the juice of ½ a lemon. Bring to a boil then simmer for 15 minutes. Remove from the heat and mash the fruit if necessary.

Add 6 cups of granulated sugar and mix thoroughly. Bring to

a boil, remove from the heat, add 3 ounces of liquid pectin. Bring to a boil for 1 full minute. Pour into hot, sterile jelly jars and seal.

Spiced Pear Jam

> 3 lbs. of ripe fruit
> Juice of 1 lemon
> 6 cups of sugar
> Spices: 4 whole cloves
>   4 sticks of cinnamon
>   ginger

Use about 3 pounds of fully ripened fruit. Peel and core then quarter. Mash the fruit with a potato masher or use your blender. Place the mix over a high heat and bring to a boil; then simmer until juice runs freely.

Force the juicy pulp through a strainer or food mill. Add the juice of one lemon, 4 whole cloves, 4 sticks of cinnamon, a small piece of ginger and 6 cups of granulated sugar. Mix thoroughly. Bring to a boil and cook at a soft boil for 20–30 minutes. Adjust the flavor to suit your sweet tooth by adding more sugar.

When the mix begins to thicken, pour off into hot, sterile jelly jars. Then seal.

Pickled Pears

> 2 quarts of choke pears
> 2 lbs. of brown sugar
> 2 cups of cider vinegar
> Spices: 2 sticks of cinnamon
>   6 whole cloves

Combine the sugar and vinegar in a deep saucepan. Add a spice bag with the cinnamon and cloves. Mix thoroughly. Bring the mix to a boil and cook at a soft boil for 10 minutes.

Thinly peel the choke pears and cook a few at a time in the syrup. Once all the pears have been cooked, place them into hot, sterile jars. Keep the jars hot in a water bath. Add syrup, covering the fruit and seal tightly.

Pickled Unpeeled Pears

     4 lbs. ripe choke pears
     2 cups of cider vinegar
     1 cup cold water
     4 cups granulated sugar
     Spices: 5—6 sticks of cinnamon
                8 whole cloves
                1 tablespoon whole allspice

Wash the pears, remove the flower ends, but leave the stems. They make very nice handles. Place the fruit in a deep saucepan, cover with water and bring to a boil. Cook at a soft boil for 10 minutes. Remove from the heat and drain off the water. Remove the fruit and using a toothpick, prick several holes into the skin of each pear.

Make up a syrup of 2 cups of cider vinegar, 1 cup of cold water, 4 cups of granulated sugar and mix thoroughly. Add the spice bag, bring to a boil, and cook at a soft boil for 5 minutes. Add the pears and boil for 10 minutes. Remove from the heat, cover and allow the mixture to stand overnight.

The next morning, remove the spice bag and place the mixture over a high heat. Bring to a boil for 1 full minute. Pack the pears into hot, sterile jars. Fill with hot syrup and seal.

Ginger Pears

     3 lbs. of semi-ripe choke pears
     1 quart of water
     2 tablespoons of cider vinegar
     2 cups of granulated sugar
     1 cup of white vinegar
     Spices: 10 whole cloves
                8 2-inch sticks of cinnamon
                2-inch piece ginger

Wash, peel, core and quarter 3 lbs. of semi-ripe choke pears. Place the peeled fruit into a saucepan, cover with 1 quart of water and 2 tablespoons of cider vinegar.

Make up a syrup of 2 cups of granulated sugar (3 cups if you have a real sweet tooth), 1 cup of white vinegar and 1 cup of cold water. Add the spice bag, cover the mixture and bring to a boil for 5 minutes.

Drain the pears and add the hot syrup mix. Cover, lower the heat and simmer for 6—8 minutes. Remove the spice bag. Using a serrated spoon, remove the pears and pack into hot, sterile jars. Pour the hot syrup over the fruit and fill to within ½ inch of the top. Seal and place into a hot water bath for 10 minutes then wipe and store.

Pear Relish

> 3 lbs. of semi-ripe choke pears
> 1 large green pepper
> 1 large red pepper
> 1 small red pepper
> 1 large onion
> 1½ cups of cider vinegar
> 1½ cups of granulated sugar
> ½ teaspoon canning salt

Wash, peel, core and quarter 3 lbs. of semi-ripe choke pears. Chop into small sections a desired size. Drain.

Fine chop the peppers and onion. Combine the peppers, onion and fruit in a large saucepan. Add 1½ cups of cider vinegar, 1½ cups of sugar and ½ teaspoon of canning salt. Mix thoroughly and bring to a boil. Cook at a soft boil for 20 minutes.

Pack the fruit sections in pint containers, cover with the sauce, cover and place in a process water canner. Process for 10 minutes at boiling point.

Remove, seal, cool, tighten seals and store.

Crab Apple

CRAB APPLE
(Pyrus sp.)

A small tree, the Crab Apple is found primarily in the northern states. It has a range from Ontario and New England south to Florida. There are several species of Crab Apple, often all can be found in the same area. Narrow-leaved Crab Apple *(P. angustifolia)* can be found growing from southern New England south to Florida and west to Kansas. The Western Crab Apple *(P. ioensis)* has a range throughout the mid-western U.S. The American Crab Apple *(P. coronaria)* ranges from Ontario south to the Carolinas and west to Iowa.

The leaves are narrow or ovate, dark green, toothed margins and up to 3 inches in length. The blossoms are white-pink and yield a small 1–1½ inch fruit that resembles an apple and is colored red when fully ripened. The fruit is somewhat sour, but is excellent when cooked or pickled.

Most wild Crab Apple trees bear an abundance of fruit and are ready for harvest just after the first frost, which helps to color the small fruit. The Crab Apple has high concentrations of natural pectin just below the skin layer. When selecting fruit it is wise to select partially ripe Crab Apples as they yield a much better flavor than fully ripe fruit, and more pectin.

The Siberian Crab Apple *(P. baccata)* is a small, cultivated tree used primarily as an ornamental species. In recent years it has escaped to the nearby wilds and other areas where Crab Apples might be found. The fruit is abundant and quite edible, although somewhat smaller.

Crab Apple Jelly

> 5 lbs. partially ripe fruit
> 5 cups of water
> 8 cups of granulated sugar

Select 5 pounds of partially ripened crab apples, discarding any soft or rotten fruit. Remove the blossom ends and stems. Cut the fruit into thin slices, leaving the peels and cores intact. Place the fruit into a deep saucepan, add 5 cups of water, cover and simmer over a low heat for 10 minutes. Use a hand masher and crush the fruit completely, producing a juicy sauce. Allow the mix to simmer for 5—10 minutes longer.

Remove from the heat, strain through a jelly bag, gently squeezing the pulp but do not force any of the pulp into the juice. Save the pulp and make jellied apple butter.

Recover the juice, place into a saucepan, add 8 cups of granulated sugar and stir constantly over a moderate heat until sugar is thoroughly dissolved. Then bring to a boil for 1 full minute. Pour the jelly into hot, sterile jars and seal.

Crab Apple Mint Jelly

> 5 lbs. of partially ripe crab apples
> 5 cups of water
> 8 cups of granulated sugar
> 1 bunch of fresh mint leaves

Use the preceding recipe for crab apple jelly. After you have completely dissolved the sugar, add the mint leaves, but first bruise the leaves and stems. Then tie them in a bundle. Pass the mint bundle through the hot crab apple sauce until you obtain the desired mint flavor. The longer the mint remains in the sauce, the stronger becomes the flavor.

When the desired mint flavor is obtained, remove the mint leaves and bring the mixture to a boil for 1 full minute. Then pour the sauce in hot, sterile jars and seal.

Crab Apple-Quince Jelly

> 3 quarts crab apples
> 3 pints of quince
> 1 cup of sugar per cup of juice

Select, wash and stem 3 quarts of partially ripened crab apples. Remove the blossom ends and cut the fruit into slices.

Wash, peel and cut into slices 3 pints of ripe quince. Cook the fruit in separate saucepans until soft and the juice flows freely. Separately pass the juicy sauce through jelly bags. Combine the two juices in a deep saucepan. For each cup of juice add 1 cup of granulated sugar.

69

Cook the combined sauce until the sugar has completely dissolved. Bring to a full boil for 1 minute. Pour into hot, sterile jelly jars and seal.

Crab Apple Preserves

    2 quarts of crab apples
    1 sliced juice orange
    1 sliced lemon
    1 cup of sugar per cup of sauce

Wash and remove the stems and flower remnants from 2 quarts of partially ripened crab apples. Slice the fruit into quarters, core and peel. Place the peelings in a deep saucepan and just cover with water. Add 1 thinly sliced juice orange and lemon. Mix thoroughly and simmer until peelings are soft.

Strain the mixture, saving the juice. Place the juice in a saucepan, add the citrus fruit and crab apple slices. Add 1 cup of granulated sugar to each cup of sauce. Mix thoroughly.

Bring the mixture to a boil. Reduce the heat and simmer until fruit softens. Pour the mixture through a strainer. Boil the syrup down until it is quite thick. Then add the fruit to hot, sterile jars, cover with the hot syrup and seal. Allow 1 month before using.

Crab Apple Pickles I

    6 lbs. crab apples
    1 quart cider vinegar
    2 cups of sugar
        Spices: 2 sticks of cinnamon
               1 tablespoon whole cloves

Select 6 pounds of uniformly colored crab apples and more or less uniform in size. Wash, but do not remove the stems or flower remnants. Use the apple intact. Puncture the skin a few times with a toothpick.

Make up the spice bag. Place the apples in a deep saucepan, add 1 quart of cider vinegar, 2 cups of granulated sugar and suspend the spice bag in the solution. Place over a moderate heat, bringing the mixture to a slow boil. Cook at a soft boil for 20 minutes, stirring occasionally.

Remove the fruit, pack into hot, sterile jars, cover with the hot syrup and seal. Allow the pickled fruit to age for 1 month before serving.

Crab Apple Pickles II

> 6 lbs. crab apples
> 2 cups cider vinegar
> 2 cups wine vinegar
> 2 lbs. brown sugar
> Spices: 1 stick of cinnamon
> 1 tablespoon of whole cloves
> 1 tablespoon of whole allspice

Wash 6 lbs. of fully ripened and uniform sized crab apples. Into a saucepan place 2 cups of cider vinegar, 2 cups of wine vinegar, 2 lbs. of brown sugar and the spice bag. Bring the mixture to a boil.

Puncture the skin of each of the crab apples and add to the boiling sauce. Cook at a soft boil for 20 minutes, stirring occasionally. Remove the fruit, pack into hot, sterile jars, cover with the hot syrup and seal. Allow the pickled fruit to age for 1 month before serving.

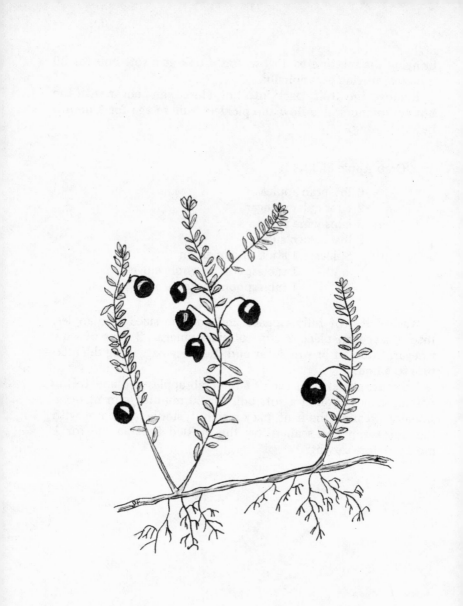

Cranberry, Bog

CRANBERRY, BOG
(Vaccinium macrocarpus)

This wonderful, small bog plant is a relative of the Blueberry. We are all familiar with the commercial varieties that so decorate the table at Thanksgiving and Christmas. Few people realize that this wonderful fruit grows wild in boggy areas throughout northeastern United States and southern Canada.

The Bog Cranberry is a creeping, somewhat brittle vine, 3 or 4 inches to 12 inches in length. The short stubby branches have oval, evergreen leaves. The fruit is a berry; bright red when ripe, firm and about ½ to 1 inch in size.

Mountain Cranberry *(V. Vitis-Idaea)* can also be used much in the same manner as the Bog Cranberry. As the name indicates, this small but abundant scraggly plant is usually found at higher elevations. The leaves are similar to the Bog Cranberry and it bears bright red fruit. The fruit is much smaller and less tart than the Bog Cranberry and tends to become quite pulpy when it remains on the vine too long.

Cranberry Jelly

> 4 cups of cranberries
> 2 cups of water
> 2 cups of sugar

Wash 4 cups of ripe cranberries and drain. Place the cranberries into a deep saucepan, add 2 cups of water and bring to a boil. Cook at a soft boil until berries soften and pop their skins. Remove from the heat and strain. The sauce will be somewhat pulpy.

Bring the sauce to a boil, add 2 cups of granulated sugar and boil until the sugar is completely dissolved.

Skim off the foam, and pour the delightful sauce into hot, sterile jelly jars and seal.

Cranberry-Grape Jelly

> 1 cup of ripe cranberries
> 2 cups of ripe grapes
> 1 tablespoon of lemon juice
> 3 ounces of liquid pectin

73

You will need the juices of wild cranberries and grapes. Boil 1 cup of ripe cranberries in ½ cup of water for 20 minutes. Squeeze the juicy sauce through a sieve. Then pass the juice through 2 layers of cheese cloth or use a jelly bag.

At the same time, boil 2 cups of washed grapes in 1 cup of water until all the grapes pop. Strain the pulpy juice through a sieve, and then pass the juice through cheese cloth or a jelly bag.

Mix the 2 juices together, adding 1 tablespoon of lemon juice and 3 ounces of liquid pectin. Bring to a boil and cook for 5 minutes. Then pour into hot jelly jars and seal.

Cranberry-Crab Apple Jelly

1 quart of ripe cranberries
5—6 medium size crab apples
1 cup sugar per cup of juice

Place 1 quart of fully ripened cranberries into a deep saucepan, add a little water and cook until berries pop and the juice runs freely.

Wash, stem, de-flower and core 5—6 medium sized partially ripened crab apples. Cut the fruit into eighths. Cook until fruit softens, then crush with a hand masher.

Strain both fruits through jelly bags, recovering the juice. Do not squeeze the pulp.

Combine one cup of cranberry juice to each cup of crab apple juice. Place in a deep saucepan, add 1 cup of granulated sugar to each cup of juice. Bring the mixture to a boil and cook until sugar completely dissolves. Then cook the mixture over a slow boil until it begins to thicken. Test for jelling with the "sheet" test.

Pour into hot, sterile jars and seal.

Cranberry-Apple-Quince Jelly

25 medium crab apples
10 medium quince
1 quart cranberries
1 cup sugar per cup of juice

Wash, stem, de-flower and core 25 medium sized crab apples. Place into a saucepan, add the cranberries. Just cover with water and cook over a moderate heat for 30 minutes.

Separately cook 10 medium sized quinces for about 20 minutes. They should first be washed, stemmed, and de-flowered. Once fully cooked, combine the cooked fruits, juice and all. Mix thoroughly then strain to extract the juice. Strain the juice through a jelly bag and measure. Place the juice in a saucepan.

Add 1 cup of granulated sugar to each cup of juice. Bring the mix to a boil and cook for 20 minutes or until jelly "sheets". Skim off the foam and pour into hot, sterile jars and seal.

Cranberry Conserve

> 4 cups of cranberries
> 1½ cups of water
> ¼ lb. seedless raisins
> ½ cup chopped walnut meats
> 1 orange
> 6 cups of sugar

Wash and stem 4 cups of fully ripened cranberries. Add the berries to a saucepan with 1½ cups of water. Cook until the berries have softened and burst. Stir to keep the bottom berries from burning.

Add ¼ lb. of chopped seedless raisins, ½ cup of chopped walnut or pignut meats, 1 orange, chopped and 6 cups of granulated sugar. Mix thoroughly. Cook the concoction for 25 minutes. Skim off the colorful surface, pour the sauce into hot, sterile jars and seal.

Cranberry Sauce

> 4 cups of cranberries
> 2 cups of water
> 1 orange
> 2 cups of sugar

Place 2 cups of water, the grated rind of 1 orange and 2 cups of granulated sugar into a saucepan, mix thoroughly and cook over a moderate heat for 5 minutes.

Add the cleaned cranberries and cook until berries pop their skins. When cooking is complete, place the sauce in a bowl and chill. Serve chilled. It will be slightly runny and not jelled.

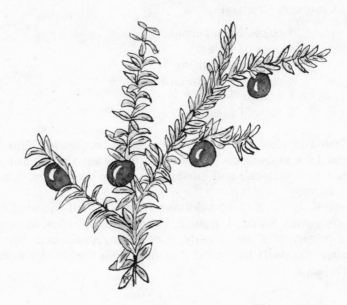

Crowberry

CROWBERRY
(Empetrum nigrum)

The Crowberry is a low spreading evergreen bush or shrub. Highly branched, it has leaves that are small, slender and needle-like. The plant bears small, almost inconspicuous purple flowers, usually in the axils of the leaves. The small, delicate flowers yield a drupe, a juicy berry-like fruit with a purple-black color. The fruit matures in the early fall and may remain on the shrub throughout the early winter months. It is somewhat tasteless and mealy when eaten raw. Cooking enhances the flavor.

The Crowberry can be found throughout the Arctic region, Newfoundland and south along the mountains of New York, New England and California. It thrives in small patches of soil in rock outcrops.

Crowberry Jelly

>   1 quart ripe crowberries
>   1 tablespoon lemon juice
> 1½ cup sugar per each cup juice
>   3 ounces pectin

Wash 1 quart of fully ripened berries. They may appear dehydrated, but they are still useable. Place the berries in a saucepan, add a little water and cook until the berries pop and the juice runs freely.

Allow the juicy sauce to simmer 15 minutes. Pour the mixture through a jelly bag.

Measure the juice, add to a saucepan, and stir in 1 tablespoon of lemon juice. Add 1½ cups of granulated sugar to each cup of juice, mix thoroughly and bring to a boil. Add 3 ounces of liquid pectin and boil for 3 minutes.

Remove the colorful foam, pour into hot, sterile jars and seal. The finished jelly will have an umber or bright brown color.

Crowberry Jam

    1 quart of ripe berries
    1 teaspoon lemon juice
    4 cups sugar
    3 ounces pectin

Wash and stem 1 quart of fully ripened berries. Place into a saucepan and crush the berries with a potato masher. Cover the berries with a little water and cook over a low heat for 15 minutes. Remove from the heat and strain through a food mill. This will remove the seeds and skins. You may add the skins to the sauce if you wish.

Place the pulpy juice into a saucepan. Add 1 teaspoon of lemon juice, 4 cups of granulated sugar and mix thoroughly. Bring to a boil for 3 full minutes.

Skim off the brown colored foam. Pour into hot, sterile jars and seal.

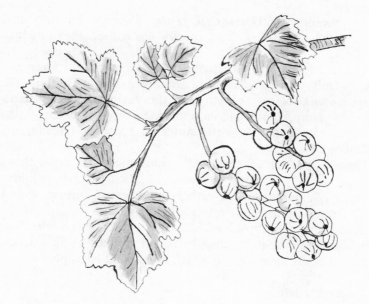

Wild Currants

CURRANTS
(Ribes sp.)

A shrub; the wild Currants are almost vine-like with low hanging branches that root freely where they touch the ground. The fruit of the Red Currant *(R. satinum)* is juicy, red, smooth, translucent and tart. It is an upright shrub, with heart shaped leaves with fine lobes and often hairy on the undersides. The shrub may attain heights of 5 feet and bear fruit in late June or early July.

The Swamp Red Currant *(R. triste)* is similar, but may have leaves of 3 to 5 lobes. This species has a foul smell but fruit is edible.

The Black Currant *(R. nigrum)* has escaped cultivation and bears fruit similar to the American Black Currant *(R. americanum)*, black, smooth and translucent. These currants grow in damp, moist places and range through much of the mountainous areas of North America, southern Canada, and northern U.S.

Canadian Black Currant *(R. hudsonianum)* grows from Alaska, south to Iowa, Oregon and Michigan. The Golden Currant *(R. aureum)* is a rather tall western currant with a range from California north to southern Alaska.

There are many more wild Currants and Gooseberries, but the above are most commonly found in greater abundance. The fruit of all these species is tart, edible, but lacks pectin.

Currant Jelly

> 2 quarts ripe fruit
> 1 cup of water
> 2 cups of sugar

Select 2 quarts of ripe currants (red, black or white), wash and stem. Place the fruit in a deep saucepan and add 1 cup of water. Bring to a boil and cook at a soft boil for 15 minutes. The fruit will develop a whitish color when ready.

Strain the mixture through a jelly bag. Do not squeeze the pulp through the jelly bag as this will make the jelly cloudy and not clear.

Collect the juice, place into a saucepan and heat to boiling. Add 2 cups of granulated sugar and 3 ounces of liquid pectin. Bring to a boil for 5 minutes, stirring constantly. Skim off the colorful foam, pour into hot, sterile jars and seal.

Spiced Currant Jelly

> 4 cups of ripe currants
> ¼ cup of cider vinegar
> ¼ cup of water
> Spices: 1 teaspoon ground cloves
> 1 teaspoon ground cinnamon
> 6 cups of sugar
> 3 ounces pectin

Wash and clean 4 cups of fully ripened currants. Crush in a deep saucepan or blender. Add ¼ cup of cold water and ¼ cup of cider vinegar. Add the spices and mix the contents thoroughly. Place over a high heat, bring to a boil, stirring constantly. Then simmer over a low heat 10 minutes, keeping the pan cooked.

Add 6 cups of granulated sugar and stir well. Bring to a hard boil until sugar dissolves. Add 3 ounces of liquid pectin, bring to a boil for 1 full minute.

Remove from the heat, skim off the foam, pour into hot, sterile jars and seal.

Currant-Raspberry Jelly

> 4 cups of ripe currants
> 4 cups of raspberries
> ¾ cup of sugar per cup of sauce

Wash and clean 4 cups of each fruit and mix in a saucepan. Crush or use the blender. Bring the mixture to a boil. Allow to simmer for 10 minutes. The skin of the currants will appear colorless when ready.

Strain the cooked mixture through a jelly bag. Measure out 8 cups of juice and add ¾ cup of granulated sugar to each cup of juice. Boil the mixture until the sugar is completely dissolved. Add 3 ounces of liquid pectin and hold at a boil for 1

81

minute. Skim off the foam, pour into hot, sterile jars and
seal.

Currant-Mint Jelly

2 quarts ripe currants
1 cup of water
3½ cups of mint leaves
¼ cup of vinegar
3½ cups of granulated sugar
3 ounces of pectin

Select 2 quarts of fully ripened wild currants and wash in
cold water. Drain and stem, being careful not to damage the
fruit. Place in a deep saucepan, bring to a boil and simmer for
15 minutes. The fruit will become colorless when ready. Strain
through a jelly bag, but be careful not to squeeze any of the
pulp though.

Add 1 cup of water, 3½ cups of fresh mint leaves, ¼ cup of
vinegar, 3½ cups of granulated sugar and mix thoroughly.
Bring to a hard boil for 3 full minutes, stir constantly. Add 3
ounces of liquid pectin and boil for 5 minutes.

Skim off the foam and strain out the mint leaves. Pour into
hot, sterile jelly jars and seal.

Currant-Honey Jam

3 quarts ripe currants
6 cups sugar
½ cup of honey

Wash and stem 3 quarts of fully ripened currants and place
in a deep saucepan. Crush a few currants to provide a little
cooking juice. Bring to a slow boil for 1 full minute. Add 6
cups of granulated sugar, mix thoroughly and simmer for 20
minutes.

Slowly fold in ½ cup of heated honey and mix thoroughly.
Simmer for 5 minutes. Remove from the heat, pour into hot,
sterile jelly jars and seal.

Elderberry, Black

ELDERBERRY
(Sambucus canadensis)

The common Elderberry or Black-berried Elder is one of the most abundant wild fruits of the northern United States. Considered a shrub, this plant may attain a height of 10 feet or more. It can be found growing along the edges of roadways, railroads, hedgerows, wetland, edges of woodlands and thickets. When found, there are usually several bushes in a single area.

The twigs are somewhat brittle with a large white pithy center. The leaves are compound, large with 5—11 leaflets, coarse toothed margins and elliptical in shape.

The flowers are borne in large white clusters or umbels, about 4—6 inches in diameter. It is best to locate Elderberry when the flowers are in bloom, noting the location. Return in the fall to harvest the large clusters of black berries. The clusters are so heavy with ripe fruit that their weight pulls the branches downward.

The fruit is sweet with a deep purple to black color, about ¼ inch in diameter and containing 3—4 nutlets as seeds. The flowers open in June and the fruit ripens in late summer or early autumn. The fruit has a high concentration of vitamin C, 100 mg. of ascorbic acid for each ounce of fruit.

All parts of this shrub contain the poison, hydrocyanic acid. The poison is destroyed by cooking. Red Elderberry *(S. pubens)* is considered poisonous and should not be used as cooking does not destroy enough of the toxin.

Elderberry Jelly

    3 lbs. elderberries
    ½ cup lemon juice
    6 cups sugar
    6 ounces pectin

Wash and stem 3 pounds of fully ripened elderberries. Place in a saucepan and crush. Place the juicy mess over a moderate heat and cook for 15 minutes. Strain the sauce through a jelly bag and recover 3 cups of juice. Place into a saucepan. Add

½ cup of lemon juice and mix thoroughly. Add 6 cups of granulated sugar, bring to a boil until the sugar is completely dissolved.

Add 6 ounces of liquid pectin, bring to a boil for 1 full minute, and stir constantly. Skim off the colorful foam, pour into hot, sterile jelly jars and seal.

Elderberry-Apple Jelly

2 quarts elderberries
4 medium cooking apples
2 quarts of water
1 cup of sugar per cup of juice
1 tablespoon of lemon juice

Crush 2 quarts of fully ripened elderberries, cleaned and stemmed. Place the berries in a deep saucepan.

Wash, stem and remove the blossom remnants of 4 medium size cooking apples. Cut the apples into quarters, add to the berries and mash with a potato masher. Add 2 quarts of cold water and simmer for 20 minutes. Stir occasionally to prevent the bottom from burning.

Strain the mixture through a jelly bag. Measure the juice, place into a saucepan and add 1 cup of granulated sugar to each cup of juice. Stir in 1 tablespoon of lemon juice and bring the mixture to a boil for 1 full minute. Lower the heat and cook until the sauce "sheets". Then pour into hot, sterile jelly jars and seal.

Elderberry Jam

4 cups of crushed fruit
3 cups of sugar
3 ounces pectin

Crush enough fully ripened elderberries to obtain 4 cups of crushed fruit. Cook at a moderate heat for 15 minutes and then strain through a food mill, removing the seeds. Place the pulpy sauce into a saucepan, add 3 cups of granulated sugar and mix thoroughly. Cook until the sugar completely dissolves.

Add 3 ounces of liquid pectin, bring to a full boil for 1 minute. Skim off the colorful foam, pour into hot, sterile jelly jars and seal.

Elderberry-Crab Apple Jam

> 1 quart of ripe elderberries
> 1½ quarts of ripe crab apples
> Juice of 2 oranges
> Juice of 1 lemon
> ½ lemon rind
> 2 orange rinds

Wash, core and stem the crab apples (do not pare), and cook until soft and the juice flows. Add 1 quart of fully ripened elderberries, the juice of 2 oranges, the rind of 2 oranges and 1 lemon. Mix thoroughly. Next add the granulated sugar and mix thoroughly.

Bring the mixture to a boil and continue to cook at a slow boil, for 30 minutes, or until the mixture begins to thicken. Remove from the heat, strain, pour the sauce into hot, sterile jelly jars and seal.

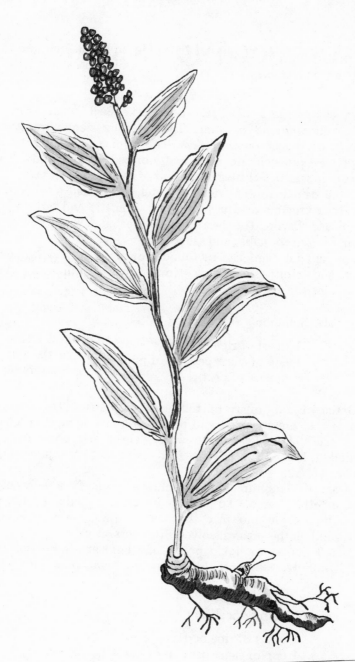

Solomon's Seal, False

FALSE SOLOMON'S SEAL
(Smilacina racemosa)

False Spikenard or False Solomon's Seal grows from a fleshy underground rhizome. The so-called stem may attain heights of 2 feet on the curve. The stem may bear 5–10 or more leaves which are oval and pointed at the ends. The flowers appear in a cluster at the end of the stem.

These dainty flowers yield a cluster of freckled pink berries that turn bright red. They are quite aromatic and tart with a sharp acid flavor. The berries can be eaten raw, as you find them, or used for jellies and sauces.

This unique plant can be found growing in shaded, wooded areas and moist soils from Nova Scotia south along the mountains to Georgia.

False Solomon's Seal Jelly

> 1 quart of ripe berries
> 1 cup of sugar per cup of juice
> 3 ounces of pectin

Gather 1 full quart of fully ripened berries. Do not use berries that are speckled and pink. Wash and stem, then place in a saucepan, add a little water, cover and cook over a moderate heat until all the fruit pops and the juice runs freely.

Strain the mixture through cheese cloth or a jelly bag. Measure the liquid. To each cup of juice add 1 cup of granulated sugar and mix thoroughly. Bring to a boil and cook until all the sugar dissolves. Stir constantly.

Add 3 ounces of liquid pectin and hold at a hard boil for 1 full minute. Skim off the bright red foam, pour into jelly jars and seal.

False Solomon's Seal Jam

> 1 quart of ripe berries
> 1 cup of sugar per cup of sauce
> 3 ounces of pectin

Wash and stem 1 quart of fully ripened berries. Place in a saucepan, add a little water, cover and cook over a moderate heat until all berries pop and the juice flows freely.

Strain the cooked fruit through a food mill. Measure out the juicy pulp, add 1 cup of granulated sugar to each cup of juicy pulp. Bring to a boil, stirring constantly, until all the sugar dissolves.

Add 3 ounces of liquid pectin, hold at a hard boil for 1 full minute. Stir constantly. Skim off the foam, pour the mix into hot, sterile jelly jars and seal.

False Solomon's Seal Sauce

    4 cups of ripe berries
    1 grated rind of 1 orange
    2 cups of water
    2 cups of sugar

Place 2 cups of water, the grated rind of 1 orange and 2 cups of granulated sugar into a saucepan, mix thoroughly and cook over a moderate heat for 5 minutes.

Next add washed and stemmed, 4 cups of fully ripened berries. Cook until the berries begin to pop. When cooking is complete, place the sauce in a food mill and strain out the seeds. Place the sauce in a bowl and chill in the refrigerator. Serve chilled.

False Solomon's Seal Cocktail

Crush as many berries as desired. Place into a saucepan, cover and cook at a moderate heat for 10 minutes.

Strain the mixture through a jelly bag. Collect the juice, add 1 teaspoon of lemon juice and the desired amount of sugar. Stir thoroughly until all the sugar is dissolved. Place into the refrigerator and serve chilled.

Grape, Fox

GRAPES, WILD
(Vitis sp.)

There are many different species of wild grapes that are found throughout Canada and the United States. In the northeastern United States and Canada, the Fox Grape *(V. labrusca)*, the Summer Grape *(V. aestivalis)*, the River Grape *(V. vulpina)*, and the Winter Grape *(V. bicolor)* are the most common. They range from New Brunswick south to Maryland.

Sweet Winter Grape *(V. cinerea)*, Red Grape *(V. palmata)*, Muscadine *(V. rotundifolia)*, and the Sand Grape *(V. rupestris)* are common in the southern portions of the United States from Texas east to Florida and the Carolinas.

The Fox Grape *(V. labrusca)* is perhaps the most common and is usually found growing in thickets, climbing over small trees and shrubs. The fruit is in sparse clusters, ¾ of an inch in size, and dark purple in color.

The fruit ripens in September or early October and is covered with a fine coating of wild yeast; thus giving it a musky odor. When using wild grapes for jellies or jams, it is best to select them partially ripened as they have a higher concentration of natural pectin and a much better flavor.

Wild Grape Jelly

> 5 lbs. of wild grapes
> ½ cup of water
> 8 cups of sugar
> 2 ounces of pectin

Stem and wash 5 pounds of wild grapes. Use a ratio of 3 pounds partially ripened grapes and 2 pounds of fully ripened grapes. Place into a deep saucepan and crush with a potato masher. Add ½ cup of water and bring the mixture to a boil. Cover and simmer for 15 minutes.

Strain the cooked fruit through a food mill, then through a jelly bag. Save the pulp for grape butter. Place the juice in a saucepan, add 8 cups of granulated sugar and bring to a boil. Add 2 ounces of liquid pectin and again boil for 1 full minute. Skim off the delightful foam, pour into jelly jars and seal.

Spiced Wild Grape Jelly

     5 lbs. of grapes
     8 cups of sugar
     ½ cup of water
     Spices: 1 teaspoon of ground allspice
              1 teaspoon of whole cloves
              1 teaspoon of ground cinnamon
     2 ounces of pectin

Use any of the wild grapes. Stem and wash 3 pounds of partially ripened and 2 pounds of fully ripened grapes. Place in a deep saucepan and crush using a hand masher. Add the spices, ½ cup of water and mix thoroughly. Cover, bring to a boil and simmer for 15 minutes.

Strain the mixture through a food mill; then a jelly bag. Save the pulp to make a spicy grape butter. Place the grape juice into a saucepan, add 8 cups of granulated sugar and boil until the sugar completely dissolves. Then add 2 ounces of liquid pectin, hold at a boil for 2 full minutes. Skim off the colorful foam, pour into hot, sterile jelly jars and seal.

Wild Grape-Herb Jelly

     3 lbs. of wild grapes
     ½ cup of water
     1 cup of sugar per each cup of juice
     3 ounces of pectin
     1 bundle of herbs

Stem and wash 3 pounds of any of the local wild grapes. Use only fully ripened grapes. Crush a few at a time in a deep saucepan. Add ½ cup of water and bring the mixture to a boil, then simmer for 10 minutes.

Strain the mixture through a food mill; then a jelly bag. Place the juice into a saucepan and suspend a desired herb into the juice. Tie into a bundle an herb such as mint, marjoram etc. Swish the herb bundle through the juice. The longer the herb remains in the juice the stronger the herb flavor becomes.

Remove the herb bundle, add 1 cup of sugar to each cup of juice and bring the sauce to a boil for 1 full minute. Add 3 ounces of pectin and cook at a boil for 1 full minute. Skim off the foam, pour into hot, sterile jelly jars and seal.

Grape Jam

3 lbs. of wild grapes
½ cup of water
1 cup sugar per cup of juice
3 ounces pectin

Stem and wash 3 pounds of both partially and fully ripened wild grapes. Crush a few at a time in a deep saucepan. Add ½ cup of water and bring to a boil. Simmer the sauce for 10 minutes.

Strain the mixture through a food mill. Measure the juicy pulp into a saucepan and add 1 cup of granulated sugar to each cup of juicy pulp. Boil for 1 minute, then add 3 ounces of liquid pectin and boil again for 1 full minute. Skim off the colorful foam, pour into hot, sterile jelly jars and seal.

Grape Conserve

3 quarts of wild grapes
1 cup of water
4 cups of sugar
1 cup orange pulp
2 cups of seedless raisins

Stem and wash 3 quarts of any fully ripened wild grapes. Peel the skins and place them into a saucepan with 1 cup of water. Cook for 15 minutes. Cook the peeled grapes without water for 10 minutes. Remove the mixture and press through a food mill or sieve.

Combine the two juices, add 4 cups of granulated sugar, 1 cup of orange pulp, 2 cups of seedless raisins and cook over a medium heat for 40 minutes. Stir frequently.

Skim off any foam, pour into hot, sterile jars and seal. Allow to age 1 month before serving.

Ground Cherry

GROUND CHERRY
(Physalis sp.)

The Ground Cherry has been cultivated for over 100 years in North America as a garden vegetable and as a floral ornament. It has, as have many plants, escaped to the wild.

It thrives along fence rows, waste areas and abandoned farm lands. There are two widely used species, the Mexican Ground Tomato *(P. ixocarpa)* and the Ground Cherry *(P. heterophylla)*.

The plant attains a height of 2 feet, usually sprawling over the surface of the earth. The greenish-yellow flowers are borne in the leaf axils, yielding a fruit that is enclosed in a calyx or husk, similar to a Japanese Latern. The berry, when ripe, is either a yellow or red color and about ½ inch in diameter.

The cherry or tomato can be eaten raw when ripe, cooked as jams, sauces or in pies. The unripened fruit is undesirable because of the repungent taste and can also cause intestinal problems.

The stem is either erect or sprawling and sometimes hairy and sticky. The leaves alternate on the stem, the margins are bluntly toothed and range up to 3 or 4 inches in length.

The Ground Cherry has a growth range extending from New Brunswick south to Florida and west to Colorado. There are some 25 or more related species that can be found within this general area of growth.

Ground Cherry Jam

2 quarts of fruit
Juice of 1 lemon
Grated peeling of 1 lemon
1 cup of water
8 cups of sugar
6 ounces of pectin

Use fully ripened ground cherries. Remove the husks and stem remnants, wash, and place in a deep saucepan. Add the juice of 1 lemon, grated peeling of 1 lemon, 1 cup of water, and mix with the fruit thoroughly. Boil for 5 minutes, stirring constantly.

95

Add 8 cups of granulated sugar and 6 ounces of liquid pectin. Mix well, bring to a hard boil for 2 minutes. Skim off the colorful orange foam, pour into hot, sterile jars and seal.

Ground Cherry Preserves

    1 quart of fruit
    3 cups of sugar
    1 lemon, sliced
    1 cup of water
    1 stick of cinnamon

Make up a syrup of the following ingredients: 1 cup of cold water, 3 cups of granulated sugar, 1 stick of whole cinnamon, 1 lemon, sliced extremely thin. Mix well and bring to a boil and cook for 10 minutes.

Add 1 quart of washed fruit and boil until the skins of the fruit look transparent. Then place the mixture in a cool place, covered, and allow to stand overnight.

Heat the mixture the next morning to boiling point, pour into hot, sterile jars and seal.

Ground Cherry Relish

    4 cups of fruit
    ¼ cup of honey
    ½ cup of vinegar
    1 cup of seedless raisins
    2 teaspoons mixed spices
    4 tablespoons of brown sugar

Husk and wash 4 cups of fully ripened fruit. Place in a deep saucepan, add all of the above ingredients and bring to a boil. Cook for 5 minutes and stir constantly. Simmer until thick. Pour into hot, sterile jars and seal.

Hackberry

HACKBERRY
(Celtis occidentalis)

A tree; Hackberry will attain heights of 100 feet or more. There are several species of Hackberry found throughout the United States. Sugar or Hackberry *(C. occidentalis)* ranges from New England south to the Carolinas and west to Oklahoma. Western Hackberry *(C. reticulata)* is found in and around Colorado. Southern Hackberry *(C. mississippiensis)* is found throughout the southern United States.

The leaves resemble that of the American Elm, unequal sided, with saw-toothed margins. Light olive green upper surface with a much lighter under surface and may range in length of 2–4 inches.

The fruit is a cherrylike drupe, about ⅓ of an inch in diameter with an orange to blue-black color. The pulp is quite sweet and leaves a very pleasant after taste. The large seed takes up most of the volume, making it necessary to collect large amounts of the fruit if you wish to make jellies or jams.

Hackberry Jelly

        1 quart ripe berries
        ½ cup sugar per cup of juice
        3 ounces pectin

Select 1 quart of fully ripened berries, wash and stem. Place into a saucepan, add a little water, and cook over a moderate heat until the fruit pops. Crush with a food masher and continue to cook for 5 minutes. Remove from the heat and strain through a jelly bag. Do not squeeze the pulp.

Measure the juice and add ½ cup of granulated sugar to each cup of juice. Bring to a boil until it dissolves, stirring constantly. Add 3 ounces of liquid pectin and boil for 2 minutes. Skim off the beautiful blue foam, pour into hot, sterile jars, and seal.

Hackberry-Sage Jelly

        1 quart ripe fruit
        1 cup of sugar per cup of juice
        Sage
        3 ounces liquid pectin

Wash and stem 1 quart of fully ripened fruit. Place in a deep saucepan, add a little water, and cook over a moderate heat until fruit pops. Strain the sauce through a jelly bag.

Measure the juice, add 1 cup of granulated sugar to each cup of juice. Add either fresh or dried sage stems and leaves. If you use fresh plant sprigs, first bruise the leaves, tie several sprigs together and suspend in the juice. If dried sprigs are used, make-up a small, porous spice bag.

Place the prepared sauce over a cook. The longer the sage remains in the juice, the stronger the flavor. When the desired flavor has been attained, remove the spice and bring the mixture to a boil for 1 full minute. Add 3 ounces of liquid pectin and continue to boil for 1 minute. Skim off the foam, pour into hot, sterile jars and seal.

Hackberry-Clove Jelly

> 4 cups of ripe fruit
> ½ cup of water
> 5 cups of sugar
> 12 whole cloves

Wash and stem 4 cups of fully ripened fruit. Place into a deep saucepan. Add ½ cup of water, 12 whole cloves, and 5 cups of granulated sugar. Mix thoroughly. Place the mix over a low heat and cook for 30 minutes. Strain the mixture through a jelly bag. Continue to cook until the jelly "sheet" test is positive, then pour into hot, sterile jars and seal.

Hobblebush

HOBBLEBUSH

(Viburnum alnifolium)

One of the many Viburnum species, Hobblebush or American Wayfaring Bush, can be found growing in the wild from New Brunswick south to the Carolinas and west to Michigan. It is most common in mountainous areas, especially in open fields. It will attain a height of 10–15 feet, with branches that grow parallel to the ground and often take root where they touch the ground.

The leaves are large; 4–8 inches across, heart-shaped, and with fine toothed margins. The flowers are white, small in clusters of 6–8 inches in diameter. The flowers yield a cluster of berries that are, at first pink, then red, and eventually turn blue when they are fully ripened. The fruit is quite sweet and edible when ripe, which is usually in early autumn. When the berries dehydrate on the vine and shrivel up, they can still be harvested. You can rehydrate by soaking in warm water. These berries can be used as easily as fresh fruit. Do not intentionally look for berries in this particular condition. Birds usually eat them long before any can dehydrate.

Hobblebush Jelly

> 3 lbs. of ripe fruit
> 1 cup of sugar per cup of juice
> ½ tablespoon lemon juice
> 3 ounces liquid pectin

Select and wash only fully ripened berries. Place the fruit in a saucepan, and crush with a potato masher. Bring the juice to a boil and simmer for 15 minutes. Strain the juicy pulp through a jelly bag.

Measure the juice and add 1 cup of granulated sugar to each cup of juice. Mix thoroughly and add ½ tablespoon of lemon juice. Bring the mixture to a boil and add 3 ounces of liquid pectin. Bring to a boil for 2 full minutes. Skim off the reddish colored foam, pour into hot, sterile jelly jars and seal.

Hobblebush-Apple Jelly

> 3 cups of apple juice
> 3 cups of berry juice
> 7 cups of sugar
> 2 tablespoons lemon juice

Select enough partially ripe apples to make up 3 cups of apple juice. Remove the stems and flower remnants. Slice into quarter sections, add just a little cooking water, cover and bring to a boil. Simmer for 15 minutes. Crush the apple sections with a masher and continue to cook for another five minutes. Remove from the heat and strain the mixture through a jelly bag. Recover 3 cups of apple juice.

Place enough cleaned hobblebush fruit into a saucepan to yield 3 cups of juice. Add a little cooking water and bring to a boil, then simmer for 15 minutes. Strain the juicy pulp through a jelly bag. Recover 3 cups of juice.

Blend the apple and hobblebush juice in a saucepan and cook for 5 minutes. Add 7 cups of granulated sugar and the lemon juice, mix thoroughly, then bring to a boil. Boil for 3 full minutes, stirring constantly. Skim off the colorful foam, pour into hot, sterile jelly jars and seal.

Hobblebush Jam

> 3 lbs. of ripe fruit
> 1 cup of sugar per cup of pulp

Clean and stem 3 pounds of fully ripened berries, place into a saucepan and simmer until the fruit pops the skins. Strain the juicy pulp through a food mill. This will remove the seeds and skins. Add some of the skins to the pulp if so desired.

Measure the pulp and add 1 cup of granulated sugar to each cup of sauce. Bring to a boil, add 3 ounces of liquid pectin and boil for 2 full minutes. Stir constantly. Skim off the colorful foam, pour into hot, sterile jars and seal.

Honey locust

HONEY LOCUST
(Gleditsia triacanthos)

A large tree; the Honey locust attains heights of 100 feet or more. It has a growth range from New England south to Florida and west to Texas. This very popular ornamental tree is being planted along highways and is a part of landscaping public and industrial sites. It survives the usual forms of air pollution quite well.

This particular locust species has quite sizeable thorns along the trunk to the smaller branches. The leaves are twice compounded, 4 to 8 inches long. The leaflets are in pairs, up to 1½ inches long, blunt ends, shiny dark green above with yellow underneath. The margins have inconspicuous, rounded teeth.

The flowers are small, greenish-white, narrow clusters, 2 inches long and generally appear in late spring. These flower clusters yield a purple-brown colored, twisted pod that ranges in size upwards to 15 inches. It is filled with large, flat seeds. The pods are thin, flat, and somewhat curved. They are filled with a sweet, succulent pulp that can be eaten raw or cooked. The sweet, greenish-yellow pulp is scraped from the pod and then cooked. The large, flat seeds can also be harvested, dried or roasted, then ground to a pulp and used as a soup base. The pods turn a maroon to brown color when completely ripened.

Honey locust Jelly

    4 cups of ripe pulp
    Sugar
    3 ounces liquid pectin

Gather 20 or so fully ripened pods. Slice the pods open and scrape out the sweetish, green to yellow pulp. Place the pulp into a saucepan and add ½ cup of water. Bring to a boil, then simmer for 15 minutes. Strain the juicy pulp through a jelly bag and recover the juice. Depending on its sweet taste, add ½ to 1 cup of granulated sugar to each cup of juice.

Mix thoroughly, bring to a boil until the sugar thoroughly dissolves. Add 3 ounces of liquid pectin, boil for 2 full minutes.

Skim off the yellowish foam, pour into hot, sterile jelly jars and seal.

Honey locust Spiced Jelly

    4 cups of pulp
    ⅓ cup of water
    ¾ cup of cider vinegar
    3 cups of sugar
    3 ounces liquid pectin
      Spices: 1 tablespoon ground cinnamon
              ½ tablespoon ground allspice
              6 whole cloves

Scrape out the sweet pulp of 20 or more ripe pods. Recover 4 cups of pulp, place into a deep saucepan, adding ⅓ cup of water, cider vinegar, 3 cups of granulated sugar, and the spices. Mix thoroughly, bring to a boil and simmer for 30 minutes, stirring occasionally.

Pour the mixture through a jelly bag, recover the spicy juice and place into a saucepan. Bring to a boil, add 3 ounces of liquid pectin, then boil for 2 full minutes. Skim off the foam. Pour into hot, sterile jelly jars and seal.

Honeysuckle

HONEYSUCKLE
(Lonicera sp.)

This is a wide spreading shrub, usually found growing in open, sunny areas such as fields or forest margins. Several species abound throughout much of the United States. Many of these wild shrubs have been adapted for ornamental planting in landscape settings, primarily because of the abundance of flowers and fruit.

Tartarian Honeysuckle *(L. tatarica)* can be found growing from Maine south to Kentucky and attains a height of 5–10 feet. American Fly-Honeysuckle *(L. canadensis)* ranges from Quebec south to New England and west to Minnesota. Swamp Fly-Honeysuckle *(L. oblongifolia)* grows from New Brunswick south to Pennsylvania and west to Minnesota. It attains a height of 2–6 feet. Mountain Fly-Honeysuckle *(L. caerulea)* attains a height of 1–5 feet and ranges from Newfoundland west to Alaska, south to Pennsylvania, Minnesota and the mountains of California.

The leaves are small, simple, ovate, sharp-pointed, finely or irregularly toothed and range up to 5 inches in length. This shrub bears small, funnel shaped flowers in great abundance. The fruit is a fleshy, round berry, small and generally red or orange in color.

One small shrub may yield upwards of 20 quarts of fruit which should provide you with many hours of enjoyable work. The trick is to constantly observe the shrubs and pick the fruit before the birds help themselves. Do save some for our feathered friends. Let them share in your bounty.

Honeysuckle Jelly

> 2 quarts ripe berries
> ½ cup of water
> 1 cup sugar per cup of juice
> 3 ounces liquid pectin

Collect, sort and wash 2 quarts of fully ripened berries. Place into a saucepan, add ½ cup of water and bring to a boil. Simmer for 15 minutes. Remove from the heat and strain through a jelly bag.

Recover the juice, measure, place into a saucepan and add 1 cup of granulated sugar to each cup of juice. Mix thoroughly and boil until sugar thoroughly dissolves.

Add 3 ounces of liquid pectin; boil for 1 full minute, stirring constantly. Skim off any foam, pour into hot, sterile jelly jars and seal.

Honeysuckle Jam

> 2 quarts ripe berries
> ½ cup of water
> 1 cup of sugar per cup of pulp
> 3 ounces liquid pectin

Wash and sort 2 quarts of fully ripened berries. Place in a saucepan and crush with a potato masher. Add ½ cup of cold water and bring to a boil. Simmer for 5 minutes. Strain the mixture through a food mill.

Recover, measure the juicy pulp, add 1 cup of granulated sugar to each cup of pulp and bring to a boil. Add 3 ounces of liquid pectin and boil for 1 full minute. Skim off the foam, pour into hot, sterile jelly jars and seal.

Buckthorn

INDIAN CHERRY
(Rhamnus caroliniana)

This tall shrub is also locally known as Buckthorn or Carolina Buckthorn. It attains heights of 10–30 feet. The branches are covered with a fine hair when young. It is quite common in swamps and other types of wetlands from New England south to Florida and west to Kansas and Texas.

The leaves are large and alternate on the stems. They are olive green in color, elliptical, pointed at the tip, smooth with fine toothed margins. The flowers are almost inconspicuous, yellow-green in color and have 5 petals. The flowers appear after the leaves, usually in late May or early June. They yield a spherical fruit, ⅓ inch in diameter, at first red then turning purple black. There are three large seeds and they are bitter to the taste. The fleshy fruit is sweet when fully ripened. The fruit generally is ripe in mid to late September, depending on local conditions. The mature fruit lacks in pectin.

Indian Cherry Jelly

> 12 cups of ripe fruit
> 3 cups of water
> 6 cups of sugar
> 6 ounces liquid pectin

Clean and stem 12 cups of fully ripened fruit. Place into a deep saucepan, add 3 cups of water, bring to a boil and simmer for 15 minutes or until fruit pops its skin. Mash with a potato masher and simmer for 5 minutes.

Strain the mixture through a jelly bag. Collect 3 cups of juice, place into a saucepan, add 6 cups of granulated sugar and mix thoroughly. Bring to a boil until all the sugar is dissolved. Add 6 ounces of liquid pectin and boil for 2 full minutes. Skim off the colorful blue foam, pour into hot, sterile jars and seal.

Spiced Indian Cherry Jelly

  12 cups of ripe fruit
   3 cups of water
   6 cups of sugar
   6 ounces liquid pectin
     Spices: 6 whole cloves
              2 sticks of cinnamon
              1 tablespoon of ground allspice
   1 teaspoon of lemon juice

Stem and wash 12 cups of fully ripened fruit. Place into a saucepan, add 3 cups of water and the spices. Bring to a boil and cook until the fruit pops the skins. Allow to simmer for 15 minutes.

Strain the mixture through a jelly bag, recover 3 cups of juice, and place into a saucepan. Add 6 cups of granulated sugar and 1 teaspoon of lemon juice. Bring to a boil until all the sugar dissolves. Add 6 ounces of liquid pectin and hold at a boil for 1 full minute. Skim off the colorful foam, pour into hot, sterile jelly jars and seal.

Indian Cherry Jam

  14 cups of ripe fruit
   2 cups of water
   6 cups of sugar
   6 ounces liquid pectin

Stem and clean 14 cups of fully ripened fruit. Place into a saucepan, add the water and bring to a boil. Simmer for 15 minutes. Mash the uncooked fruit with a potato masher. Continue to simmer for 5 minutes.

Strain the juicy pulp through a food mill. Recover 3 cups of juicy pulp and place in a saucepan. Add 6 cups of granulated sugar, mix thoroughly and bring to a boil for 1 full minute. Add 6 ounces of liquid pectin and boil for 1 full minute. Skim off the foam, pour into hot, sterile jelly jars and seal.

Irish Moss

IRISH MOSS
(Chondrus crispus)

Known locally by many names, among them Carrageen, Salt Rock Moss and Rock Moss. An alga, it attains lengths of 1—2 feet and grows in large clumps. It is commonly found along the North Atlantic shores, usually on tidal rocks. It has a growth range from Newfoundland south to the Carolinas.

The fronds range in length from 6—24 inches, with thick stems. They are leathery, smooth, olive colored to black when found in deeper water.

They can be gathered at anytime of the year. Rather insipid when eaten raw, the flavor is greatly enhanced when cooked. The cooked fronds will yield about 60% gelatin which is quite nutritious.

Irish Moss Jelly

> 3 lbs. fresh algae
> 1 cup sugar per cup of juice
> Juice of ½ lemon

Collect about 3 pounds of fresh Irish Moss algae. Rinse in fresh water to remove all traces of salt. Chop the fronds into small 1—2 inch pieces and place into a saucepan with 2 quarts of boiling water. Cook until the water begins to thicken. Remove from the heat, strain and measure the juice. To each cup of juice add 1 cup of granulated sugar. Mix in a saucepan, add the juice of ½ lemon and bring the mixture to a boil. Stir constantly. Boil for 1 full minute. Pour the mixture into hot, sterile jelly jars and seal.

Manzanita

MANZANITA

(Arctostaphylos manzanita)

Considered an evergreen shrub, Manzanita will attain heights to 10 feet. Usually it can be found growing in mountainous areas of Oregon, south to Southern California. It is also planted as an ornamental shrub in much of Eastern United States where it has escaped to the wilds in many places.

This shrub thrives in wet, humid areas. It is an erect and somewhat brittle looking plant. The leaves are evergreen, smooth, oblong, small and with entire margins.

The branches are covered with a fine hairy fuzz. The flowers are white and are in dense clusters that yield reddish-brown berries. The berries are somewhat pulpy and acrid when eaten raw, but cooking greatly improves this condition. Only use fully ripe and fleshy berries, do not use dehydrated fruit.

Manzanita Jelly

> 2 quarts of ripe berries
> 1½ cups sugar per cup of juice
> 3 ounces liquid pectin

Collect 2 quarts of fully ripened berries and wash thoroughly to remove the grime. Place into a saucepan, add 1 cup of cold water and bring to a boil. Simmer for 15 minutes. Strain the mixture through a jelly bag.

Recover and measure the juice, add 1½ cups of granulated sugar to each cup of fruit juice. Bring to a boil for 1 full minute, add 3 ounces of liquid pectin and boil for 2 full minutes. Skim off the umber colored foam, pour into hot, sterile jelly jars and seal.

Manzanita Jam

> 2 quarts of ripe fruit
> 1 cup of water
> 1½ cups sugar per cup of pulp
> 3 ounces liquid pectin

115

Collect 2 quarts of fully ripe berries, wash thoroughly and place in a deep saucepan. Add 1 cup of cold water, bring to a boil and then simmer for 15 minutes. Remove from the heat and strain through a food mill. This will remove the seeds and skins.

Measure the juicy pulp, add 1½ cups of granulated sugar to each cup of juicy pulp and bring to a boil. Add 3 ounces of liquid pectin, boil for 1 full minute and stir constantly. Skim off the foam, pour into hot, sterile jelly jars and seal.

Manzanita Conserve

4 cups of ripe fruit
1½ cups of water
¼ lb. chopped seedless raisins
½ cup chopped nut meats
1 chopped orange
10 cups sugar

Wash and stem 4 cups of ripe berries. Add to a saucepan with 1½ cups of cold water. Cook until the berries have softened and the juice runs freely. Add the raisins, nut meats, the chopped orange and 10 cups of sugar. (You may use 8 cups of sugar, depending on your taste.)

Mix the ingredients thoroughly and cook the mixture about 25-30 minutes or until thickening takes place. Skim off the surface foam, if any. Pour into hot, sterile jelly jars and seal.

Manzanita Cider

1 quart ripe berries
1 quart of cold water

Wash and stem 1 quart of fully ripened berries, place into a saucepan, add 1 quart of cold water, bring to a boil and simmer until berries soften. Crush with a potato masher and continue to simmer for 5 minutes.

Remove from the heat, strain through a jelly bag. Recover the juice, (add a little sugar if you desire) and serve chilled. The juice is acid, as is apple cider, but very spicy and quite pleasant.

116

Ash, Mountain

MOUNTAIN ASH
(Sorbus sp.)

There are three well known species of Mountain Ash; American Mountain Ash *(S. americana)*, Mountain Ash *(S. scopulina)*, and European Mountain Ash *(S. aucuparia)*. *S. americana* has a range from Labrador south along Eastern Canada and the United States to the Carolinas. *S. scopulina* ranges from Labrador and Alaska south to Pennsylvania and Utah. *S. aucuparia* is a transplanted native of Europe. It is widely planted throughout North America as an ornamental and has successfully escaped to the surrounding wilds.

A small tree, the Mountain Ash has twigs that are fuzzy, compound leaves and flowers that are in round topped clusters. The compound leaves have 9–15 leaflets and turn reddish in the autumn. The fruit is a berry, ½ inch wide, and quite waxy. The fruit is in heavy drooping clusters. They are bright red in the American Mountain Ash, orange in the European Mountain Ash when mature, and they have a very unpleasant odor. Before using, the fruit should be carefully cleaned in hot water to remove the sticky substances and attached debris.

European Mountain Ash is easily located along highways and streets as it is not harmed by most auto pollution. All Mountain Ash fruit contains high concentrations of natural pectin; so additional pectin is not required.

Mountain Ash Jelly

> 2 lbs. ripe fruit
> 2 cups of water
> 1 cup of sugar per cup of juice

Select 2 pounds of fully ripened fruit, clean by rinsing in hot water. Remove blossom and stem ends. Place in a deep saucepan, add 2 cups of cold water and simmer for 15 minutes or until fruit softens. Remove from the heat and crush the cooked fruit with a potato masher. Cook for 5 minutes. Strain through a jelly bag.

Measure the collected juice, place in a saucepan and add 1 cup of granulated sugar to each cup of juice. Bring the mixture to a boil for 1 full minute, stirring constantly. Remove from the heat, pour into hot sterile jelly jars and seal.

Mountain Ash Jam

> 2 lbs. of ripe fruit
> 1 cup of sugar per cup of pulp

Select 2 pounds of fully ripened fruit. Wash thoroughly in hot water and remove the blossom and stems. Place the fruit into a deep saucepan, mash with a potato masher and cook the sauce for 15 minutes. Remove from the heat and pour the juicy pulp through a food mill. This will remove the seeds and skins.

Place the juicy orange pulp into a saucepan and add 1 cup of granulated sugar to each cup of juicy pulp. Mix well, bring to a boil, stirring constantly for 1 full minute. Pour into hot sterile jelly jars and seal.

Mountain Ash Marmalade

> 3 lbs. of ripe fruit
> 2 tablespoons lemon juice
> 1 orange
> 6 cups of sugar

Wash in hot water 3 pounds of fruit. Remove the stems and blossom ends. Chop fruit into small sections. Place in a deep saucepan, add 2 tablespoons of lemon juice, 1 orange diced in small sections, skin and all. Mix thoroughly. Bring to a boil, remove and add 6 cups of granulated sugar. Mix thoroughly. Bring to a boil for 2 minutes. Pour or spoon the mixture into hot sterile jelly jars and seal.

Red Mulberry

MULBERRY
(Morus rubra)

There are several species of Mulberry found throughout the United States. The Red Mulberry *(M. rubra)* is perhaps the most common, being found in the Eastern United States. It grows as a tree to a height of 50 feet. The leaves are simple, alternate on the stem and have variable shapes similar to the Sassafras. Some of the leaves may contain as many as five different lobes.

Bright red berries are produced in July, depending on local conditions. The berry is made up of numerous druplets, forming a fleshy fruit that is about 1 inch in length and ½ inch wide. The fruit is tasty when fully ripened; whereas the green, unripened fruit is somewhat bitter. The ripe berries can be used for sauces, jellies, jams, tarts, pies or just eaten raw by the handful. A delicious treat.

White Mulberry *(M. alba)* is similar to Red Mulberry with a fruit that is almost white and somewhat sweeter. In some instances, Black Mulberry *(M. nigra)* can be found in the wilds of the southeastern United States. Its black colored fruit is sweet and prized for cultivation.

Mulberry Jelly

> 2 quarts ripe mulberries
> 1–2 cups granulated sugar
> 3 ounces liquid pectin

Wash 2 quarts of fully ripened mulberries. Remove the short stems. Place into a deep saucepan, add a little cooking water, and bring to a boil. Simmer for 15 minutes. Crush the fruit with a potato masher. Strain the sauce through a jelly bag.

Recover the juice and measure. If you prefer jellies that are tart, only add 1 cup of granulated sugar to each cup of juice. Add 1½ to 2 cups of sugar if you wish a sweeter jelly. Mix thoroughly and bring the mixture to a boil.

Add 3 ounces of liquid pectin, mix thoroughly and bring to a boil for 1 full minute. Skim off the colorful foam, pour into hot, sterile jelly jars and seal.

121

Mulberry Jam

2 lbs. ripe mulberries
1–2 cups granulated sugar
3 ounces liquid pectin

Wash thoroughly 2 pounds of fully ripened mulberries. Add to a deep saucepan, add a little cooking water and bring to a boil. Simmer for 20 minutes, keeping the pot covered. Remove from the heat and strain the juicy pulp through a food mill. This will remove the seeds and skins.

Recover and measure the juicy pulp, add 1–2 cups of granulated sugar to each cup of sauce, depending on your sweet tooth. Mix thoroughly, bring to a boil for 1 minute. Add 3 ounces of liquid pectin, mix thoroughly, and boil for 1 full minute. Skim off the colorful foam, pour into hot, sterile jelly jars and seal.

Mulberry Conserve

4 cups ripe fruit
1½ cups of water
¼ lb. seedless raisins
1 chopped orange
½ cup finely chopped nut meats
10 cups of granulated sugar

Wash and stem 4 cups of fully ripened fruit. Place into a saucepan, add 1½ cups of cold water, and bring to a boil. Simmer for 10 minutes. Crush the cooked berries with a potato masher, add ¼ pound of chopped seedless raisins, 1 chopped orange, with the seeds removed, and 10 cups of granulated sugar. Mix the sauce thoroughly. Bring to a boil, cook for 20 minutes and then add ½ cup of finely chopped walnut meats. Simmer the mixture for an additional 10 minutes. Stir constantly. Remove from the heat, skim the surface, pour into hot, sterile jelly jars and seal.

Nannyberry

NANNYBERRY
(Viburnum lentago)

A tall shrub; Nannyberry is usually round topped with crooked branches. It attains heights of 10–20 feet and is common in wooded areas, stream banks, and wet thickets. It has a range from Hudson Bay south to Pennsylvania and along the Appalachian Mountains to Georgia. It can be found growing as far west as Iowa and Missouri.

The leaves have a deep lustrous green color, lighter beneath, oval shaped with margins of fine teeth. The flowers are very small, white, and in large clusters that may range up to 6–8 inches across. The flowers appear in June, yielding dark blue fruit that is covered with a yeast bloom.

The fruit is oval, ½ inch in diameter and upwards to 1 inch in length. It is edible raw and the pulp is quite tasty and sweet. The berries hang in rather large clusters and can often be found on the branch during winter months. The dried fruit of fall can be rehydrated and used as easily as the summer fruit.

Nannyberry Jelly

> 4 quarts of ripe fruit
> ½ cup of sugar per cup of juice
> 3 ounces pectin

Wash and stem 4 quarts of fully ripened fruit. Place into a saucepan and cook over a moderate heat until the fruit pops. Remove from the heat and pour the juicy sauce through a jelly bag.

Measure the juice and add ½ cup of granulated sugar to each cup of juice. Place over a high heat, bring to a boil until the sugar completely dissolves.

Add 3 ounces of liquid pectin and boil for 1 minute. Skim off the beautiful colored foam, pour into hot jelly jars and seal.

Spiced Nannyberry Jelly

    4 cups of ripe fruit
    ½ cup of water
    ¾ cup of cider vinegar
    1 tablespoon ground cinnamon
    1 teaspoon ground allspice
    6 whole cloves
    5 cups of granulated sugar

Wash and stem 4 cups of fully ripened berries, place into a saucepan with ½ cup of water, ¾ cup of cider vinegar, the spices and 5 cups of granulated sugar. Mix the ingredients thoroughly. Place over a low heat and cook for 30 minutes.

Pour the cooked sauce through a jelly bag. Recover the sauce, pour into hot, sterile jelly jars and seal.

Nannyberry Jam

    4 quarts ripe fruit
    ½ cup of sugar per cup of sauce
    3 ounces liquid pectin

Wash and stem 4 quarts of fully ripened berries. Place into a deep saucepan and cook over a moderate heat for 10 minutes. Then mash the fruit with a potato masher. Strain the pulpy sauce through a food mill. This will remove the skins and seeds.

Measure the juicy pulp, add ½ cup of granulated sugar to each cup of sauce and bring to a boil. Add 3 ounces of liquid pectin and boil hard for 1 full minute. Stir constantly. Skim off the colorful foam, pour into hot, sterile jelly jars and seal.

Oregon Grape

126

OREGON GRAPE
(Mahonia aquifolium)

Commonly known as Holly Grape, the Oregon Grape is an evergreen shrub that has leaves that resemble holly leaves. A low growing shrub, it seldom exceeds 4 feet in height. It can be found growing in the wilds from British Columbia south to California. It is commonly grown as an ornamental hedge shrub and has therefore escaped to the wilds in other parts of the United States.

The leaves are compound, holly-shaped, tough, leathery, spine tipped margins and usually has 5–9 leaflets. The leaves are quite glossy and very attractive. During cold weather the shiny green leaves take on a very attractive bronze color.

During the early spring the plant bears small short clusters of yellow flowers, usually at the tip of each of the branches. These brightly colored flowers yield edible blue colored berries, which resemble small grapes, hence the name. Although the fruit is somewhat pulpy, it can be made into excellent jellies and jams.

The State flower of Oregon; it gives the appearance of blue-berried holly, though it is not related. A related species, Dwarf Oregon Grape *(M. aquifolium compacta)* is widely used as a small, ground hugging ornamental shrub. The berries are also blue, similar to grapes and are edible. Both shrubs contain fair amounts of pectin in the ripe fruit.

Oregon Grape Jelly

8 cups of ripe berries
1½ cups sugar per cup of juice

Select only fully ripened fruit. Wash and stem 8 cups and place into a deep saucepan. Crush the fruit with a potato masher. Add a little cooking water, bring to a boil, and cook over a moderate heat for 10 minutes.

Strain the juice through a jelly bag. To each cup of juice add 1½ cups of granulated sugar. Mix thoroughly and bring the mixture to a boil. Boil until the sugar is completely dissolved. Skim off the blue colored foam, pour into hot, sterile jelly jars and seal.

Spicy Oregon Grape Jelly

4 cups of ripe berries
⅓ cup of water
¾ cup of cider vinegar
4 cups of sugar
Spices: 1 tablespoon of ground cinnamon
½ tablespoon of ground allspice
4 whole cloves

Wash and clean 4 cups of fully ripened berries. Place into a saucepan, add ⅓ cup of cold water, ¾ cup of cider vinegar, 4 cups of granulated sugar and the spices. Mix the ingredients thoroughly, bring to a boil, then simmer for 30 minutes, Stir occasionally and keep covered.

Remove the sauce from the heat and strain through a jelly bag. Bring the juice to a boil for 1 full minute. Skim off the colorful foam, pour into hot, sterile jelly jars and seal. The color will be similar to grape jelly.

Oregon Grape Jam

3 lbs. of ripe berries
2 cups of water
1 cup of sugar per cup of sauce

Wash and stem 3 pounds of fully ripened berries and place into a saucepan with 2 cups of cold water. Cook until the fruit softens and the juice runs freely. Remove from the heat and press the juicy pulp through a food mill.

Recover the juicy pulp, measure and add 1 cup of granulated sugar to each cup of juice. Mix thoroughly, bring to a boil and hold there for 15 minutes. Stir constantly.

Remove from the heat, skim off the blue foam, pour the jelly into hot, sterile jars and seal. The color will be similar to grape jam.

Papaw

PAPAW
(Asimina triloba)

A small tree, attaining heights to 50 feet, the Papaw is more often found growing as a large shrub in the wilds or as an ornamental. It is relatively common at stream edges and wet thickets. Papaw ranges from southern Canada south to Florida, Kansas and Texas. There are about 7 related species in the eastern and southeastern United States.

The leaves are large, 10–12 inches, oblong with pointed tips. The young stem growth is covered with a fine fuzz. The fruit is large, fleshy, up to 8 inches in length and 2–3 inches thick. It is brown, grows in small clusters, edible and very sweet. The pulp is sickeningly sweet. The fruits are abundant, available in late September or early October, and are best after they have been nipped by a good frost. A single fruit may weigh upwards to a pound.

The sweet pulp has a sepia brown or dull yellow color and can easily be removed by scraping the inside of the fruit hull. Be prepared to dislike this fruit; for as many as there are that like it, there are equally as many who dislike it.

Papaw Jelly

> 3 lbs. ripe papaws pulp
> ½ cup of water
> ½ cup of sugar per cup of juice
> 6 ounces liquid pectin

Select about 4 pounds of fully ripened papaws. Skin and remove the seeds. Scrape and remove 3 pounds of the sweet pulp. Place in a deep saucepan with ½ cup of cold water and bring to a boil. Simmer for 15 minutes, covered. Remove from the heat and strain through a jelly bag.

To each cup of recovered juice add ½ cup of granulated sugar and bring to a full boil for 1 minute. Add 6 ounces of liquid pectin, mix thoroughly, bring to a hard boil for 1 full minute. Remove from the heat, skim, pour into hot, sterile jars and seal.

Spiced Papaw Jam

> 3 lbs. ripe fruit pulp
> ¾ cup cider vinegar
> ½ cup water
> 6 cups sugar
>   Spices: 6 whole cloves
>   1 teaspoon ground allspice
>   1 tablespoon ground cinnamon
> 6 ounces liquid pectin

Select 4 pounds of fully ripened papaws. Remove the pulp and recover 3 pounds. Place into a saucepan with just a little cooking water, bring to a slow boil, then simmer for 10 minutes. Remove the juicy pulp and strain through a food mill.

Place the juicy pulp into a saucepan, add ¾ cup of cider vinegar, ½ cup of water, 6 cups of granulated sugar and the spices. Mix the ingredients thoroughly and cook over a low heat for 30 minutes, stirring occasionally. Do not allow the mixture to burn.

Strain the sauce through a fine sieve, add 6 ounces of liquid pectin and bring to a full boil for 1 minute. Skim, pour into hot, sterile jars and seal.

Persimmon

PERSIMMON
(Diospyros virginiana)

A native fruit, it was praised by many of the early North American settlers and explorers. De Soto made note of it in his journals in 1557.

The Persimmon is a yellow-red colored fruit when ripe and may range in size from 1–3 inches in diameter. It is very bitter or astringent when eaten green. The unripe fruit contains high concentrations of tannin, which is reduced considerably as the fruit ripens. For best results only use fully ripened fruit.

A medium sized tree, it is usually found in eastern United States, and quite common in southern Iowa and Nebraska. The leaves are oval or elliptical, about 2–6 inches long, pointed and rounded at the base. The upper surface is shiny and dark green, whereas the underneath is lighter in color and may be smooth or fuzzy.

The male and female flowers on different trees in the spring are small, ⅜ to ¾ inch long, white, and in the axil of the leaf. The fruits appear from September through November.

There are 160 species in the genus located throughout the temperate zones of the world, but mostly in Asia. Chapote *(D. texana)* has a growth range from Texas west to southern California. The fruit of both species can be eaten raw when ripe, but are best when preserved. Persimmons are orange-yellow-red when ripe, but *D. texana* fruit is a blue-black when fully ripe.

Persimmon Jelly

> 3 lbs. fully ripe persimmons
> ¼ cup of cold water
> 1 cup sugar per cup of juice
> 6 ounces liquid pectin

Stem and wash 3 pounds of fully ripened persimmons. Cut in half and remove the seeds. Crush the juicy pulp or strain through a food mill. Add ¼ cup of cold tap water, mix thoroughly. Pass through a jelly bag and recover the juice.

Place the juice in a saucepan, add 1 cup of granulated sugar for each cup of juice. Mix thoroughly and bring to a boil. Add

6 ounces of liquid pectin and boil for 1 full minute. Skim off the colorful foam, pour into hot, sterile jelly jars and seal.

Persimmon Jam

>3 lbs. of ripe persimmons
>¼ cup cold water
>1 cup of sugar per cup of pulp
>6 ounces liquid pectin

Clean 3 pounds of fully ripened persimmons. Cut them in half, removing the large, flat seeds. Crush the fruit or strain through a food mill. Add ¼ cup of cold tap water. Recover the strained juicy pulp and place into a saucepan.

Add 1 cup of granulated sugar to each cup of pulp. Bring the mixture to a boil, add 6 ounces of liquid pectin and hold at a boil for 1 full minute. Remove from the heat, skim off the foam, pour into hot, sterile jelly jars and seal.

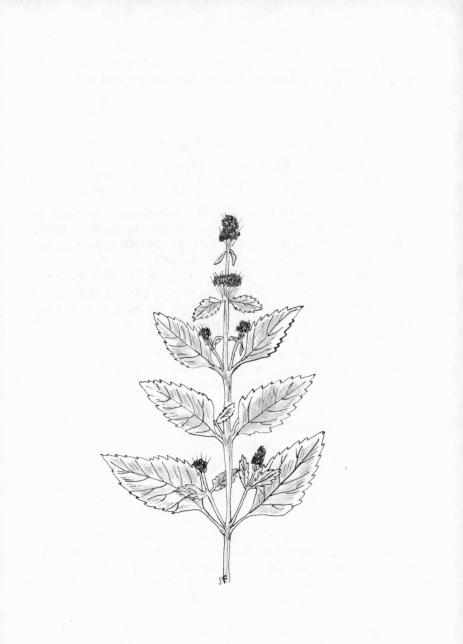

Peppermint

PEPPERMINT
(Mentha piperita)

Long used as a medicinal plant, Peppermint has been used to quell such chronic disorders as colic, nausea, and headaches. Peppermint tea is still a popular remedy for the common cold, and is commonly used as a flavoring for some cough syrups. It is also still used in soaps, candies and perfumes.

Peppermint is a member of the Mint group. It can be found growing in marshlands, stream edges and various waste lands. It grows to a height of 3 feet, with erect stems that are somewhat branched and crowded. The leaves are opposite on the stem, 3 inches long, oblate, slightly fuzzy and quite dark green. The leaves are quite distinct as there are oil glands that form spots on the leaf surfaces. The oil glands contain high concentrations of the peppermint oil.

The flowers are in thick spikes, purple in color, sometimes white. The leaves can be utilized fresh green or dried. Peppermint is an officially recognized drug.

Peppermint Jelly

> Fresh peppermint leaves
> 1 tablespoon of lemon juice
> 4½ cups of sugar
> 3 ounces liquid pectin

Collect a few handfuls of fresh peppermint leaves. Crush them in your hands, and then place the leaves into 2 quarts of boiling water. This will yield a strong peppermint tea. Boil for 10 minutes. Measure out 4 cups of the infusion, place in a saucepan, add 1 tablespoon of fresh lemon juice and bring to a boil.

Remove from the heat, add 3 ounces of liquid pectin and 4½ cups of granulated sugar. Bring to a full boil once again. Hold at a boil, stirring constantly for 1 full minute. Remove from the heat, skim, pour into hot, sterile jelly jars and seal. The jelly will lack in color, but not in flavor.

136

Peppermint-Crab Apple Jelly

 10 partially ripened crab apples
3½ cups of sugar
 4 cups of peppermint tea

Prepare a strong peppermint tea from freshly picked leaves. Measure out 4 cups of the hot beverage.

Peel 10 or so partially ripened crab apples. Cook the peels in a little water at a boil for 10 minutes.

Combine the hot brew and the juice from the apple peels in a saucepan. Add 3½ cups of granulated sugar, mix thoroughly. Bring to a boil for 1 full minute, skim the surface and pour into hot, sterile jelly jars. Seal. The color will of course resemble apple juice.

Peppermint Sauce

1 cup peppermint leaves
1 cup of vinegar (malt)
⅕ teaspoon salt
 Honey to taste

Finely ground leaves are added to 1 cup of malt vinegar and ⅕ teaspoon of canning salt. Mix thoroughly and simmer for 15 minutes. Remove from the heat, cover and allow to stand for 25–30 minutes. This will allow the flavor time to concentrate.

Strain the mixture carefully. Now add enough honey to thicken the mixture to your own taste. Usually, 2–3 ounces should be enough. You may wish to add a food coloring as it lacks in color. This delightful sauce goes well with lamb or poultry dishes. A delight when served with Cornish Hen.

Wild Plums

PLUMS, WILD
(Prunus americana)

There are several species of wild plums that can be found throughout most of the United States and Canada. The Red Plum *(P. americana)* is perhaps the most common. It grows as a small coarse shrub, to a height of 20 feet or more. It has a range from southern New England south to Florida and west to Colorado. The size of the fruit depends on locale, being much larger in the Ohio river valley. It is found growing in thickets, stream margins and forest edges.

The most famous of the wild plums is the so called Beach Plums *(P. maritima)*, which has a magical sound to its name. It is usually found along the eastern coastlines and inland as an ornamental shrub. Cape Cod is quite famous for its Beach Plum jelly.

The Wild Goose Plum *(P. hortulana)* grows in lowlands, whereas the Canada Plum *(P. nigra)* is more common in elevations of 2–4,000 feet. The fruit of the wild plum, when ripe, has a flavor that is superior to that of the commercially grown varieties. The ripe fruit can be harvested and dried in bright sunshine and will keep in a dry place for months. For the best flavor, use 20 percent red, partially ripened plums and the rest, fully ripened. 1 average wild plum yields 30 calories and 200 i.u. of vitamin A.

Wild Plum Jelly

      5 lbs. ripe plums
      1 cup of water
      7 cups of sugar
      3 ounces liquid pectin

Select 5 pounds of any of the wild plums, include some partially ripened fruit for flavor and pectin. Place into a deep saucepan and crush with a potato masher. Do not remove the pits or peels. Add 1 cup of cold tap water, bring the mixture to a boil. Simmer, covered for 15 minutes. Place in a jelly bag and remove the juice.

Measure the juice; you should recover about 5 cups. Add 7 cups of granulated sugar and bring the mixture to a boil. Add 3 ounces of liquid pectin and once again bring to a boil. Hold at a hard boil for 1 full minute. Stir constantly. Skim off the colorful foam, pour into hot, sterile jelly jars and seal. The color is spectacular.

Save the plum pulp which can be used to make an excellent plum butter.

Wild Plum Jam

    3 pints of plums
    4 cups of sugar

Wash 3 pints of fully ripened wild plums, mixing in several partially ripened plums for added flavor. Place into a saucepan and crush with a potato masher. Bring the mess to a boil; then simmer for 10 minutes. Remove from the heat and pour the hot plum sauce through a food mill. This will remove the skins and large seeds.

Place the hot juicy pulp into a saucepan, add 4 cups of granulated sugar and bring to a boil. Cook until the mixture is thick. You may wish to reduce the cooking time by adding 3 ounces of liquid pectin. Once completed cooking, pour into hot, sterile jelly jars and seal.

Wild Plum Preserves

    5 lbs. ripe plums
    1 cup of water
    1 cup sugar per cup of fruit
    2 juice oranges

Wash, then cut into halves about 5 pounds of firm but fully ripened wild plums. Remove the pits. Place the cut fruit into a deep saucepan, add 1 cup of water and to each cup of fruit add 1 cup of granulated sugar. Mix well and bring to a boil; then simmer until the sugar syrup thickens.

Select 2 ripe juice oranges, chop them into very small sections, and add to the plum sauce. Bring the mixture to a boil and then simmer for 5 minutes. Remove from the heat and pour into hot, sterile jars and seal.

Red Raspberry

RASPBERRY
(Rubus strigosus)

Two well known species of Raspberries, Red Raspberry *(R. strigosus)* and Black Raspberry *(R. occidentalis)*, can be found in fruit between July and September. Considered a native shrub from the Carolinas northward to Newfoundland, they are found upwards to elevations of 2,000 feet.

The raspberry is common to sandy type soils and burnt over lands. The canes usually grow upwards to 4–6 feet an in somewhat thick stands. The plants bear leaves that are compound, with 3–5 leaflets. They are irregular with toothed margins and have light green upper surfaces. The canes only bear fruit in the second year of growth.

The Black Raspberry, also known as Black Cap, has a much wider range of growth and usually bears more fruit. About ½ cup of freshly picked wild raspberries will yield about 3.5 calories and 80 i.u. of vitamin A and about 16 m.g. of vitamin C. It is therefore desirable to use the fruit for preserves as soon as possible, in order to preserve the flavor and nutrition.

Red Raspberry Jelly

> 3 quarts ripe berries
> 7½ cups of sugar
> 6 ounces liquid pectin

Red raspberry jelly is rare as it requires many berries in order to produce a small batch. Collect 3 quarts of fully ripened raspberries. Crush the berries in a saucepan, extract the juice with a jelly bag.

Measure out 4 cups of the colorful red juice. Add 7½ cups of granulated sugar and mix well. Bring the mixture to a boil, adding 6 ounces of liquid pectin. Bring to a hard boil for 1 minute, stirring constantly. Remove from the heat, skim off any foam, pour into hot, sterile jelly jars and seal.

Black raspberries, when used in place of red raspberries yield a spectacular color.

Raspberry Jam

2 quarts of ripe fruit
½ cup sugar per crushed fruit
6 ounces liquid pectin

Wash, crush and measure the fruit. Add sugar depending on your taste for raspberries. Use as an average between ½ to ¾ cup of granulated sugar to each cup of crushed fruit.

Place the mixture over a moderate heat and cook for 2 minutes—then bring to a boil. Add 6 ounces of liquid pectin and boil for 1 full minute. Stir constantly. Skim off the colorful foam and pour into hot, sterile jelly jars and seal.

Black Raspberry-Crab Apple Jelly

2 quarts ripe black raspberries
1 cup sliced semi-ripe crab apples
⅛ cup of water
¾ cup sugar per cup of juice

Wash and clean 2 quarts of fully ripened black raspberries. Place into a saucepan with ⅛ cup of cold tap water and cook over a moderate heat until soft.

In a separate saucepan, place 1 cup of sliced semi-ripened crab apples. Include the cores and peels. Cook until soft and juicy.

Combine the fruits and strain through a jelly bag. Measure the clear juice, place into a saucepan and add ¾ cup of granulated sugar to each cup of juice. Bring to a boil and cook for 5 minutes. Remove from the heat, skim off the foam, pour into hot, sterile jelly jars and seal.

Raspberry-Currant Jelly

1 quart of currants
1 quart of raspberries
¾ cup sugar per cup of juice
3 ounces liquid pectin

Add 1 quart of stemmed and washed currants to a saucepan. Red currants are preferred here. Crush the bottom layer of berries. This provides a little cooking juice. Add 1 quart of any raspberry, red preferred because of color. Cook over a low heat for 5 minutes or until the fruit appears soft and the skins are colorless. Once enough juice appears, pour the batch through a jelly bag.

To each cup of measured juice add ¾ cup of granulated sugar, bring to a boil. Add 3 ounces of liquid pectin and bring to a boil. Hold at a boil for 1 full minute, stirring constantly. Remove the foam, ladle into hot, sterile jelly jars and seal.

Raspberry-Strawberry Jam

1 quart ripe raspberries
1 quart ripe strawberries
6 cups of sugar
6 ounces liquid pectin

Select 1 quart each of fully ripened red raspberries and strawberries. Wash and stem. Mash the berries in a saucepan, using a potato masher. You should recover about 6 cups of mashed berries. Add 6 cups of granulated sugar to the crushed fruit, mix thoroughly and bring the mixture to a boil.

Add 6 ounces of liquid pectin and bring to a full boil for 1 full minute. Remove from the heat, skim off the foam, stirring often, pour into hot, sterile jelly jars and seal.

If wild strawberries are unavailable, certainly use commercially grown berries. But alas, the flavor is not the same. Only the wild fruit is good!

Rhubarb

RHUBARB, WILD
(Rheum rhaponticum)

A native of Southern Siberia; this plant has escaped to the wild since it was introduced to American gardens. Bucharian Rhubarb *(R. undulatum)*, a common garden species, has since escaped to the wilds—unplowed open fields or woodland margins. Both *R. rhaponticum* and *R. undulatum* may attain heights of 5—6 feet with leaves that range upward to 2 feet or more. They have broad, thick blades, and long petioles. The petioles turn from light green to dark red, rich in color with deep green foliage.

Rhubarb that has escaped to the wild can be found throughout much of northeastern United States, the Pacific coastal states, and in and around Michigan. Stalks that are well colored are highly flavored and have a delicious tart taste. Old rhubarb may be tough, pithy, and quite flavorless.

Do not eat the leaf blades which contain concentrations of oxalic acid and oxalates of potassium and calcium; all of which can be poisonous. **Only the stalk is edible.**

Wild Rhubarb Jelly

> 3 lbs. 12 inch rhubarb stalks
> 6 cups of sugar
> 6 ounces liquid pectin

Cut into small 1 inch pieces about 3 pounds of ripe 12 inch rhubarb stalks. Do not remove the outer rind. Run the chopped pieces through a food mill, then through a jelly bag. Squeeze out as much of the juice as possible. Recover about 3 to 3½ cups of juice. Place the juice into a saucepan, and add 6 cups of granulated sugar.

Bring the mixture to a boil and hold at a boil for 3—4 minutes. Then add the 6 ounces of liquid pectin, mix thoroughly and stir constantly. Bring to a boil for 1 full minute. Skim the surface and pour into hot jelly jars and seal. The jelly is almost colorless and you may want to add vegetable food color. If you do, add to the sauce just before removal from the heat.

Rhubarb-Apple Jelly

2 lbs. of 12 inch rhubarb
1 lb. of semi-ripe crab apples
6 cups of sugar
3 ounces of liquid pectin

Cut into small 1 inch pieces, 2 pounds of ripe 12 inch rhubarb stalks. Do not remove the outer rind. Run through a food mill and then through a jelly bag.

Cut into quarters, 1 pound of semi-ripened crab apples. Place into a saucepan, add a little cooking water, and simmer for 15 minutes. Pour the mess through a jelly bag and recover the juice.

Combine 2 cups of rhubarb juice and 1½ cups of crab apple juice in a saucepan, add 6 cups of granulated sugar and bring to a boil. Hold at a boil, stirring constantly for 3 minutes. Add 3 ounces of liquid pectin, bring to a boil for 1 full minute.

Skim the surface, pour into hot, sterile jelly jars and seal.

Rhubarb Jam

2 lbs. of 12 inch rhubarb
¾ cup of water
4 cups of sugar
6 ounces liquid pectin

Chop about 2 pounds of mature 12 inch rhubarb stalks in small pieces. Place into a saucepan, add ¾ cup of cold water and bring to a boil. Simmer until rhubarb sections are quite soft, 2–5 minutes. Pass the mixture through a food mill and measure out 3 cups of the juicy sauce.

Place the juicy pulp into a saucepan, add 4 cups of granulated sugar, mix thoroughly and bring to a boil. Stir in 6 ounces of liquid pectin, hold at a boil for 1 full minute. Remove from the heat, skim off the foam, pour into hot, sterile jelly jars and seal.

Rhubarb-Strawberry Jam

1½ lbs. 12 inch rhubarb
1 quart ripe wild strawberries
5 cups of sugar
6 ounces liquid pectin
¾ cup of water

147

Chop into small pieces 1½ pounds of mature rhubarb stalks. Place into a saucepan, ¾ cup of cold tap water and bring to a boil. Simmer until rhubarb is soft. Squeeze the mixture through a food mill and recover 2 cups of juicy sauce.

Crush 1 full quart of wild strawberries, add these to the rhubarb sauce. This should yield 4 cups of sauce mixture. Add 5 cups of granulated sugar, mix thoroughly and bring to a boil. Stir in 6 ounces of liquid pectin, hold at a boil for 1 full minute. Skim off the colorful foam, spoon the hot mix into hot, sterile jelly jars and seal.

Rhubarb Marmalade

> 2 lbs. 12 inch rhubarb
> Rind of 1 orange/1 lemon
> 5 cups of sugar
> Juice of 1 orange/1 lemon

Chop into small pieces 2 pounds of rhubarb stalks. Place the chopped pieces into a saucepan.

Remove the skins from 1 orange and 1 lemon. Chop them into small oblong sections. Add to the rhubarb sections and mix thoroughly. Add 5 cups of granulated sugar, mix thoroughly, cover and allow to stand overnight.

The next day, squeeze juice from the orange and lemon. Add to the mix and bring to a boil. Simmer until the mixture thickens, stirring to prevent the bottom from burning. When thick, pour into hot, sterile jelly jars and seal.

Wild Rose

ROSE, WILD
(Rosa sp.)

Considered botanically to be a shrub, there are many different species of wild roses, all of which produce beautiful and highly aromatic flowers. The flowers yield a fruit that varies in color from orange to red when ripe and resembles a small apple. The fruits also vary in size from ¼ inch to 3 inches in diameter. They may be eaten raw or used for sauces, jellies, jams, etc. The inside section of the hip is pulpy and filled with fibers that are quite bitter.

Roses are commonly found in open rocky places. They range from the Arctic, Newfoundland, Alaska south throughout most of the United States. The leaves are generally compounded, with 3 or more leaflets, leaf margins are saw-toothed, and somewhat oblong. The stems generally have spines of some type either all along the cane or scattered.

Smooth Rose *(R. blanda)* blooms early in June and is common from New Brunswick south to New Jersey. Wrinkled Rose or Beach Rose *(R. rugosa)* yields a plum size fruit, usually during August and September. Rose hips should be prepared as soon after picking as possible to ensure maximum flavor.

Rose Hip Jelly

>   3 lbs. ripe rose hips
>   2 cups of cold water
>   6 cups of sugar
>   6 ounces liquid pectin

Collect 3 pounds of fully ripened rose hips. If the rose hips have small spines on them, remove before cooking. Wash the hips, remove the "tails" and place into a saucepan. Add 2 cups of cold tap water, bring to a boil and cook over a moderate heat for 15 minutes. You may speed up this part of the cooking procedure by gently crushing the hips with a potato masher. Pour the sauce through a jelly bag, and recover 5 cups of juice.

Add the juice to a saucepan, add 6 cups of granulated sugar, mix thoroughly and bring to a boil. Add 6 ounces of liquid pectin, bring to a boil for 1 full minute. Remove from the heat, skim the foam, pour off into hot, sterile jelly jars and seal. The color of the jelly will be that of a delicate pink.

Rose Petal-Crab Apple Jelly

1 pint jar of rose petals
1 quart ripe crab apples
1½ cups of sugar per cup of juice
6 ounces liquid pectin

Fill a pint jar completely with freshly picked wild rose petals. Cover the blossoms with boiling water and cover. Keep out of bright sunshine. Allow to sit for 24 hours. This will leach the color and flavor from the blossoms. The next day strain the infusion, removing the petals.

Wash and remove the stems and the flower remnants from 1 quart of fully ripened crab apples. Cook in a little water until soft. Mash the apples, freeing the juice. Simmer for 15 minutes. Strain through a jelly bag, but do not squeeze.

Combine the rose petal juice, crab apple juice, and 1½ cups of sugar to each cup of juice. Mix thoroughly, bring to a boil for 1 full minute, or until the sugar has completely dissolved. Add the liquid pectin, hold at a full boil for 1 minute, then remove from the heat. Skim the surface, pour into hot, sterile jelly jars and seal. The color will be a dark pink. The liquid pectin is necessary because fully ripened crab apples lack in high concentrations of pectin, but yield excellent color.

Rose Petal Jelly is easily made—leave out the crab apples and substitute 1 teaspoonful of lemon juice. Adjust the liquid pectin and you can produce a delicate flavored and colored jelly.

Rose Hip-Cranberry Jelly

1 pint of rose petals
2 cups of cranberries
1 cup of water
4 cups of sugar

Fill a pint jar completely with freshly picked wild rose petals. Cover the blossoms with boiling water and cover. Keep out of bright sunshine. Allow the infusion to sit overnight for 24 hours. This will leach the color and flavor from the blossoms. The next day strain the infusion, removing the petals.

Clean and remove stems from 2 cups of wild bog cranberries and boil in 1 cup of water for about 20 minutes, or until juice runs freely. Strain through a sieve.

Place the rose petal infusion and the cranberry juice into a saucepan, bring to a boil, then add the sugar and boil until sugar has completely dissolved. Remove from the heat, skim the colorful foam, pour into hot, sterile jelly jars, and seal. You may adjust the amount of sugar to suit your taste.

Rose Hip Jam

> 3 lbs. ripe rose hips
> ½ cup of cold water
> 1 cup of sugar per cup of juice
> 6 ounces of liquid pectin

Wash and remove any spines from 3 pounds of fully ripened rose hips. Also remove any flower remnants. Place into a saucepan, add ½ cup of cold tap water and bring to a boil. Simmer until fruit breaks open and the juices run. Remove from the heat and strain the mixture through a food mill.

To each cup of juicy pulp, add 1 cup of granulated sugar. Mix thoroughly and bring to a boil. Add 6 ounces of liquid pectin, boil for 1 full minute. Remove from the heat, skim the pink foam, pour into hot, sterile jelly jars and seal.

Rose hips can be combined with a variety of fruits to obtain jams of varying flavors and colors. Reduce the number of pounds of rose hips to 1½ and substitute a fruit of 1½ pounds, and combine the pulps. The remaining recipe will serve you well.

Salal

SALAL
(Gaultheria shallon)

A small shrub, 2—3 feet in height; Salal has evergreen leaves, rounded or somewhat heart shaped, and is dark green. The small stubby branches are usually covered with a fine fuzz.

The flowers are in slender clusters, upwards to 6 inches long, borne at the tip of the branches, white with triangular lobes. These delicate flowers yield a fruit that is a small berry, black in color when fully ripened, hairy and hard. These small berries are not very palatable raw, but cooking certainly improves the flavor. The berry-like fruits are available in the fall of the year.

Native to western North America, Salal has a range from Alaska south to Southern California. It thrives in dry soils but does best where the air is quite humid. Commonly known as Salal or Shallon, it is widely used as an evergreen ornamental throughout much of the United States.

Salal Jelly

1 quart ripe salal berries
½ cup of water
1 cup of sugar per cup of juice
3 ounces liquid pectin

Collect 1 quart of the purple-black salal berries. Wash and stem, place in a saucepan, add ½ cup of water and bring to a boil. Simmer for 10 minutes or until the juice flows from the berries. Remove from the heat and strain through a jelly bag.

Recover the juice, measure, place into a saucepan and add 1 cup of granulated sugar to each cup of juice. Mix thoroughly and bring to a boil. Add 3 ounces of liquid pectin and hold at a boil for 1 full minute. Remove from the heat, skim the surface, pour into hot, sterile jelly jars and seal.

Spiced Salal Jelly

6 cups ripe salal berries
½ cup of water
1 cup of cider vinegar
6 cups of sugar
1 tablespoon ground cinnamon
1 teaspoon ground allspice
6 whole cloves
6 ounces liquid pectin

Wash and stem 6 cups of fully ripened salal berries. Place into a saucepan with ½ cup of water, 1 cup of cider vinegar, 1 tablespoon of ground cinnamon, 1 teaspoon of ground allspice, 6 whole cloves and 6 cups of granulated sugar. Mix the ingredients thoroughly. Place over a low heat and cook for 20 minutes, stirring constantly. Remove from the heat and pour the spicy sauce through a jelly bag.

Bring the juice to a boil, add 6 ounces of liquid pectin and hold at a boil for 1 full minute. Remove from the heat, skim the foam from the surface, pour into hot, sterile jelly jars and seal.

Salal Tea

2 handfuls fresh leaves
2 quarts water
Sugar to taste

Collect 2 handfuls of the fresh evergreen leaves. Dry and crush. The oil content within the leaves will remain. This provides the aroma and flavor. Add the leaves to 2 quarts of boiling water, remove from the heat and allow to steep for 10 minutes.

Strain the tea through a cloth. Add any desired amount of sugar and serve hot. Excellent brew for those cold wintry days.

Sapphireberry

SAPPHIREBERRY

(Symplocos paniculata)

A large, wide spreading, dense shrub; Sapphireberry is used in ornamental plantings where large spreading growth is desired. It has escaped to the roadsides, thickets and woodland margins. Although not too common, it can be found in semi-rural areas— where parks are located, interstate and other highway margins, and landscape screenings. It has a growth range from New England south to Florida and west to Iowa.

The plant is well named, for the small berries are sapphire blue in color. It is usually difficult to obtain enough of these colorful berries, although the shrub bears an abundance, because birds eat them as soon as they ripen. They normally remain on the shrub for about 1 week.

The flowers are small, in fuzzy clusters, and very aromatic. The leaves are dark green, oblong, pointed at the ends and the margins are entire. This unusual shrub is prized for its colorful berries but not its flowers.

Sapphireberry Jelly

> 1 quart ripe berries
> ½ cup of water
> 1 cup of sugar per cup of juice
> 3 ounces liquid pectin

Stem and wash 1 quart of fully ripened berries. Place in a saucepan, add ½ cup of water and bring to a boil. Simmer for 5 minutes, then mash with a potato masher. Cook for another 5 minutes and strain the juicy blue pulp through a jelly bag.

Recover the blue-green juice, add 1 cup of granulated sugar to each cup of juice. Mix well and bring to a boil. Add 3 ounces of liquid pectin and hold at a boil for 1 full minute. Skim off the spectacular foam. Pour into hot, sterile jelly jars and seal.

Sapphireberry Jam

> 1 quart ripe berries
> ½ cup of water
> 1 cup sugar per cup pf pulp
> 3 ounces liquid pectin

Stem and wash 1 quart of fully ripened berries. Place them into a saucepan, lightly crush with a potato masher, add ½ cup of cold tap water and bring to a boil. Simmer the fruit for five minutes.

Strain the juicy pulp through a food mill, measure and place into a saucepan. Add 1 cup of granulated sugar to each cup of juicy pulp. Mix thoroughly and bring to a boil. Add 3 ounces of liquid pectin and hold at a boil for 1 full minute. Skim off the colorful foam, pour into hot, sterile jelly jars and seal.

Sapphireberry Jelled Sauce

4 cups of ripe berries
2 cups of water
2 cups of sugar
½ cup of granulated gelatin

Clean and wash 4 cups of fully ripened berries. Add to a saucepan with 2 cups of water and bring to a boil. Simmer until berries pop and the juice flows freely. Strain through a food mill. Add 2 cups of granulated sugar and bring to a boil.

Moisten the gelatin in cold water; then add to the hot juice and stir until completely dissolved. Pour the mixture into a desired mold; chill, and serve plain or fancied up with a topping.

Sassafras

SASSAFRAS
(Sassafras variifolium)

Without a doubt this is one of the best known trees and edible wild plants of rural America. It grows along fencerows, wooded areas, thickets and abandoned lands. It thrives in dry sandy soils and has a growth range from New England south and west along the Appalachian Mountains.

The young twigs have a beautiful green bark with the older stems becoming a reddish-brown color. The leaves alternate on the stem and can be found in three distinct shapes. Greenish-yellow flowers appear in the spring, about May, and yield a drupe or berry that is blue in color.

There are two well-known species of Sassafras in North America, *(S. albidum* and *S. variifolium)* both resemble each other. The bark of the roots, stems, twigs, and the berries contain the oil oleum sassafras, which is quite spicy in flavor and has a pleasant aroma. Oleum sassafras oil has long been used as a medicinal. It is also used as a flavoring for various medicinals and candies.

Sassafras Jelly

>   6 6-inch roots or stems
>   2 quarts of water
>   1 tablespoon lemon juice
>   4½ cups of sugar
>   3 ounces liquid pectin

Collect either 6 roots, 6 inches in length and ½ inch thick, or young stems. If you use young stems and twigs, use thinner stock, but use the equivalent of 6 x ½ inch roots.

Place into boiling water and make a good strong tea. Use about 2 quarts of water and boil until a red-brown color develops. The deeper the color, the better the color for jelly. The flavor will also improve.

Strain out 4 cups of strong sassafras tea, place in a saucepan, add 1 tablespoon of lemon juice, bring to a boil, then add 4½ cups of granulated sugar. Mix thoroughly, bring to a boil, add 3 ounces of liquid pectin, and hold at a boil for 1 full minute.

Remove from the heat, skim off the surface foam, pour into hot, sterile jelly jars and seal.

Sassafras-Honey Jelly

> 4 cups sassafras tea
> 6 cups of honey
> 6 ounces of liquid pectin

Refer to the recipe on how to prepare sassafras jelly and prepare 4 cups of hot sassafras tea. Bring the tea to a boil and add 6 ounces of liquid pectin. Bring to a boil, add 6 cups of honey, and hold at a boil for 1 full minute. Remove from the heat, pour into hot, sterile jelly jars and seal.

If light colored honey is used, the color of the jelly will be much lighter than the original color of the tea. If dark colored honey, such as orange honey is used, the color of the jelly will be even darker. The honey should be strained if it is not honey from the commercial jar. The straining of fresh or wild honey will remove debris such as the hive wax.

Sassafras-Apple Jelly

> 1 pint strong sassafras tea
> 10—12 partially ripe crab apples
> 2 cups sugar per cup of combined juice

Prepare 1 pint of strong sassafras tea. Refer to the sassafras jelly recipe. Core and remove the blossom remnants from 10—12 partially ripened crab apples. Cut into eighths, place into a saucepan, add a little cooking water and place the mixture over a moderate heat. Cook until soft and juicy. Then mash the apples with a potato masher. Strain the apple juice through a jelly bag.

Combine the crab apple juice with the sassafras tea. Bring to a boil for 1 full minute. Add 2 cups of granulated sugar to each cup of combined juice and mix thoroughly. Cook until the colorful sauce passes the jelly "sheet" test. Then skim the surface, pour into hot, sterile jelly jars and seal.

Serviceberry

SERVICEBERRY
(Amelanchier canadensis)

There are some 20 different species of *Amelanchier* or Serviceberries located throughout North America, with *A. canadensis* and *A. alnifolia* the two most common.

Serviceberry, as a general term, is usually found as a large bush, 20–30 feet in height. The leaves are oval shaped, with edges finely serrated. All Serviceberries produce large clusters of sweet berries, red to purple in color and range up to ½ inch in size.

Serviceberries tend to resemble blueberries and generally grow much in the same area. They can be used as you would blueberries. The berries are excellent in flavor, when picked fresh, but tend to change flavor as they dry. The berries can be used if you find them dried on the bush, as they often can be found in late fall. The dried berries should be re-hydrated before use. One cup of ripe berries will yield about 90 calories.

The various serviceberries range throughout most of North America, from Alaska south to California, Newfoundland south to Georgia. They thrive in a variety of conditions and can be found at altitudes of 4,000 feet or more.

Serviceberry Jelly

    9 cups ripe berries
    ¾ cup of sugar per cup of juice
    ½ cup of water
    3 ounces liquid pectin

Stem and wash 9 cups of fully ripened serviceberries. Place the berries into a saucepan. Crush a few with a wooden spoon and then add ½ cup of cold tap water. Simmer the fruit over a low heat for about 10–15 minutes. Strain the cooked fruit through a jelly bag.

Recover the fruit juice, measure, and place into a saucepan. Add ¾ cup of granulated sugar to each cup of fruit juice. Mix well, place over a high heat, bring to a boil. Add 3 ounces of liquid pectin. Bring to a boil for 1 full minute. Skim the foam from the surface, pour into hot, sterile jelly jars and seal.

Serviceberry-Black Cherry Jelly

> 1 quart ripe serviceberries
> 2 lbs. ripe black cherries
> ½ cup of water
> 1 cup of sugar per cup of juice
> 6 ounces liquid pectin

Select 1 quart of fully ripened serviceberries, wash and stem. Place into a saucepan and thoroughly crush with a potato masher. Wash and stem 2 pounds of wild black cherries, then place in a separate saucepan and crush, but do not break the hard rounded stones or pits.

Combine the juicy pulp of the two fruits and add ½ cup of cold water. Place over a high heat and bring to a boil. Keep covered and allow to simmer for 10 minutes. Remove from the heat and press the mixture through a jelly bag. **Do not squeeze.**

Measure the recovered juice, place into a saucepan, add 1 cup of granulated sugar for each cup of juice. Mix thoroughly and cook over a moderate heat until the sugar has dissolved. Bring to a boil, add 6 ounces of liquid pectin, and hold at a boil for 1 full minute.

Remove from the heat, skim the foam from the surface, pour into hot, sterile jelly jars and seal.

Serviceberry Jam

> 10 cups of ripened berries
> ½ cup of water
> ¾ cup of sugar per cup of pulp
> 6 ounces liquid pectin

Wash and stem 10 cups of fully ripened berries, place into a saucepan and crush. Add ½ cup of cold tap water and cook over a moderate heat for 5–6 minutes. Add ¾ cup of granulated sugar for each cup of juicy sauce.

Place over a low heat and cook for a few minutes or until the sugar dissolves. Bring to a boil, add 6 ounces of liquid pectin and hold at a boil for 1 full minute. Remove from the heat, skim the foam, pour into hot, sterile jelly jars and seal.

Herb Spiced Serviceberries

> 15 cups of ripe berries
> 3 lbs. sugar
> 1 cup of vinegar
> 1 cup of water
> Spices: 6 whole cloves
> 1 tablespoon of whole allspice
> 1 stick of whole cinnamon
> Selected herb

Make up a syrup of 3 pounds of granulated sugar, 1 cup of vinegar and 1 cup of water. Add a spice bag as described above. Bring to a boil and cook for 10 minutes; then remove from the heat and allow to cool.

Add 15 cups of washed and stemmed serviceberries and heat to simmering. Allow to simmer until berries soften. Remove from the heat, cool quickly, and let stand overnight.

Next day remove the spice bag, spoon the fruit into hot sterile jars. Re-heat the syrup to a boil and pass a selected herb (such as tarragon, basil, or mint) through the hot syrup until you obtain the desired flavor and aroma.

Pour the herb syrup over the berries, seal the yet hot jars. Allow the spiced berries to sit for 30 days before serving. This will give the spicy herb syrup a chance to do its work.

Serviceberry Relish

> 4 cups ripe berries
> ¼ cup of cold water
> ¼ cup of cider vinegar
> 6 cups of sugar
> 1 teaspoon ground cinnamon
> 6 whole cloves
> 2 ounces of liquid pectin

Wash and stem 4 cups of fully ripened berries. Place the fruit into a deep saucepan, crush with a potato masher. Add spices, ¼ cup of cold tap water, and ¼ cup of cider vinegar. Bring the mix to a boil, stirring constantly. Place over a low heat and simmer for 10 minutes. Keep the pan covered.

Recover 4 cups of the hot sauce, place in a saucepan, add 6 cups of granulated sugar and mix well. Place over a high heat, bring to a boil. Add 3 ounces of liquid pectin, mix thoroughly. Bring to a boil for 1 full minute, skim off any foam, allow to sit for 3–5 minutes. This will prevent the fruit pulp from floating to the top. Spoon or pour into hot, sterile jelly jars and seal.

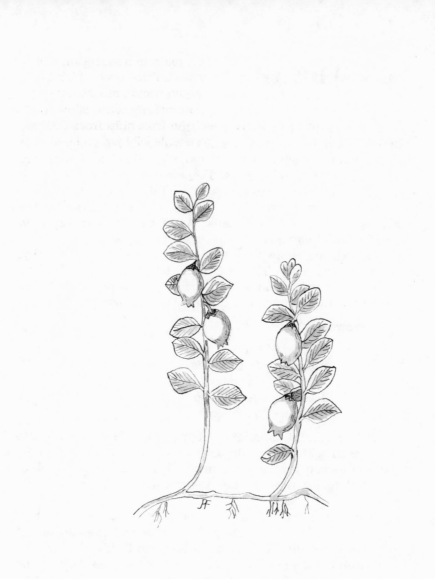

Snowberry

SNOWBERRY
(Symphoricarpos albus)

This small plant takes its name from the bright white colored berry that it bears on its slender branches. This evergreen has small branches, trailing along the ground, and the plant is usually found growing in thick mats. The woody stems are short with an abundance of small ovate leaves, ½–1 inch in length.

It has a growth range from Labrador west to British Columbia and south to Pennsylvania. Areas of growth range from conifer forests and mixed woodlands to boggy areas.

The delicate white flowers yield of course a white, fleshy, juicy but acid berry. The berries and leaves are highly aromatic with a wintergreen flavor. Have patience in collecting this delicate fruit. Even though it is sparse but well worth the effort.

Snowberry Jelly

1 quart of fruit
2 handfuls fresh leaves
1 cup of cold water
1 cup of sugar per cup of juice
3 ounces liquid pectin

Wash and bruise 2 handfuls of fresh picked leaves. Place into a saucepan with 1 cup of cold tap water and bring to a boil. Allow to steep for 15–20 minutes. This will extract much of the wintergreen flavor. Strain the hot tea, discard the leaf residue.

Wash and stem 1 quart of ripe berries, eliminate overripe fruit as it lacks flavor. Place the berries and the cup of hot snowberry tea into a saucepan. Crush the fruit and bring to a boil. Allow to simmer for 5 minutes. Remove from the heat and pour through a jelly bag. Recover the aromatic juice, measure, and into a saucepan add 1 cup of granulated sugar to each cup of hot juice. Mix thoroughly and bring to a boil.

Add 3 ounces of liquid pectin and hold at a boil for 1 full minute. Stir constantly. Skim off the foam, pour into hot, sterile jelly jars and seal. The jelly will have a light brown color. If you wish, you may add a few drops of vegetable coloring to give it a better appearance.

Snowberry Tea

Add 2 handfuls of snowberry leaves, freshly picked to 1 quart of boiling water. Bruise the leaves before placing them into the hot water. Allow the mixture to steep for 10 minutes; then strain out any leaves and other debris.

Serve either hot or chilled. This is a very pleasant wintergreen-flavored beverage.

Wild Strawberry

STRAWBERRY
(Fragaria virginiana)

There are many wild fruits that are much easier to gather than the wild strawberry, but none that have the exotic taste and aroma of this berry.

There are several wild species of the wild strawberry, among the more common is the Wood Strawberry *(F. vesca)* and the Bog Strawberry *(F. canadensis)*. All produce a similar sized berry, sweet with apparent difference in flavor. The berry is small, unlike the commercial varieties.

The Wild Strawberry ranges from Florida northward to New Brunswick, Nova Scotia, and west to Iowa. The plant is easily recognized by its compound leaves. Composed of 3 broad leaflets, they are quite saw-toothed at the margins. A low ground plant, the strawberry sends out runners which establish new plants. This type of reproduction produces thick growths of plants. They appear to do best in shaded, somewhat moist, sandy soils.

The white flowers yield a red pulpy, quite juicy fruit. They do not keep very well and easily bruise as they are picked. The fresh fruit, as well as the leaves, yield vitamin C. About ½ cup of fruit yields 44 mg. of vitamin C.

Wild Strawberry Jelly (Un-cooked)

1½ quarts ripe berries
4 cups of sugar
2 tablespoons cold water
3 ounces liquid pectin

Select and wash 1½ quarts of fully ripe wild strawberries. Place a few at a time into a saucepan and crush with a potato masher, or crush in a blender. Place the juicy sauce in a jelly bag and recover the juice.

Measure out 1¾ cups of strawberry juice into a saucepan, add 4 cups of granulated sugar, and mix thoroughly. Allow to stand for 10 minutes. Add 2 tablespoons of cold tap water, 3 ounces of liquid pectin and mix thoroughly. Stir constantly for the last 5 minutes.

171

Pour directly into freezer containers, seal tightly, and allow to set out at room temperature overnight. Freeze or use immediately.

Wild Strawberry Jelly (Cooked)

> 1 quart ripe strawberries
> 1 cup of cold water
> 2 cups of sugar
> 3 ounces liquid pectin

Remove stems and wash 1 quart of fully ripened wild strawberries. Place into a saucepan and add 1 cup of cold water. Bring to a boil and cook for 2—3 minutes. Strain the cooked sauce through a jelly bag. Recover about 2 cups of juice.

Combine 2 cups of granulated sugar, 3 ounces of liquid pectin, and the juice. Bring to a boil for 1 full minute. Skim the surface, pour into hot, sterile jelly jars and seal.

Strawberry Jam

> 2 cups wild strawberries
> ½ teaspoon lemon juice
> 3 cups sugar
> 3 ounces liquid pectin

Pick, stem, and carefully wash 2 cups of wild sweet strawberries. Place into a saucepan, add ½ teaspoon of lemon juice. Bring to a boil, add 3 cups of granulated sugar and 3 ounces of liquid pectin. Gently mix and hold at a boil for 1 full minute.

Skim off any foam, spoon into hot sterile jars, and seal.

Strawberry Preserves

> 2½ cups of fruit
> 3½ cups of sugar
> ½ teaspoon lemon juice

Wash and stem 2½ cups of freshly picked wild strawberries. Pack whole berries on the bottom of a saucepan, covering each layer with granulated sugar. Bring the mixture to a quick boil. Remove from the heat, set aside to cool at room temperature for 3—4 hours. Keep covered.

Place the fruit over a high heat, bring to a boil for a full 2 minutes. Stir gently. Remove from heat and gently spoon into hot, sterile jelly jars and seal. Be certain that you cover the fruit with the thick sauce or the fruit will dehydrate in the jars.

Strawberry-Rhubarb Preserves

> 3 6-inch sections of ripe rhubarb
> 1 quart fresh wild strawberries
> 4 cups of sugar

You may use wild or cultivated rhubarb,whichever is in season with the wild strawberries. Wash thoroughly and cut the stalks into small sections. Measure out about ½ quart. Place into a saucepan, cover with 4 cups of granulated sugar and allow the mix to stand overnight—covered.

The next day, bring the mixture to a boil. Add 1 quart of wild strawberries. Simmer for 15 minutes, stirring occasionally. Spoon into hot, sterile jelly jars and seal.

Sunshine Strawberry Preserve

> 1 quart ripe berries
> Sugar

Wash 1 quart of ripe wild strawberries. Place a layer of berries into a saucepan, cover freely with granulated sugar. Cover each layer of berries with an equal amount of sugar. Cover and allow to stand for ½ hour.

Bring to a boil, then simmer for 10 minutes. Pour the berries into a bake pan of some type and loosely cover with clear plastic sheeting of some type. Place the covered berries out into a bright sun. You may have to leave the wild berries in the bright sunshine for 1 or 2 days, until the juice forms and thickens. When ready, spoon the berries into hot, sterile jelly jars, cover with the syrup and seal.

Pickled Strawberries

> 1 quart ripe berries
> ½ cup of vinegar (white)
> 1 cup of sugar
> Ground cinnamon
> Ground cloves

173

You may use wild or cultivated strawberries. Clean the berries. Use 1 full quart. Place the berrries into a saucepan, stoneware, or porcelain. Cover each layer with a little ground cinnamon and ground cloves.

In a separate saucepan bring ½ cup of white vinegar and 1 cup of granulated sugar to a boil. Pour the syrup over the berries, cover, and allow to stand overnight.

The next day, drain off the syrup and bring to a boil. If wild strawberries are used, combine the hot syrup and the berries and bring to a boil for 10 minutes.

If cultivated berries are used, pour the hot syrup over the fruit, cover, and allow to stand for a second night. Next day, drain the syrup, bring to a boil, then pour over the berries. Boil the fruit for 20 minutes in the syrup.

When ready, spoon the cooked fruit into hot, sterile jelly jars, cover the fruit with the hot syrup and seal.

Spiced Wild Strawberries

> 1 quart ripe berries
> ½ cup of sugar
> ½ cup of white vinegar
> ½ cup of cold water
>   Spices: 6 whole cloves
>   1 stick of cinnamon
>   1 small 1-inch section ginger root

Wash, remove the greenery, and place in a saucepan. Combine in a separate saucepan ½ cup of granulated sugar, ½ cup of white vinegar, ½ cup of cold tap water, and the spices. Bring to a boil and cook for 5–6 minutes. Add the strawberries and bring to a boil.

Spoon the strawberries into hot, sterile jars. Cover with the hot spicy syrup and seal. Allow to age for 5–6 weeks before serving.

174

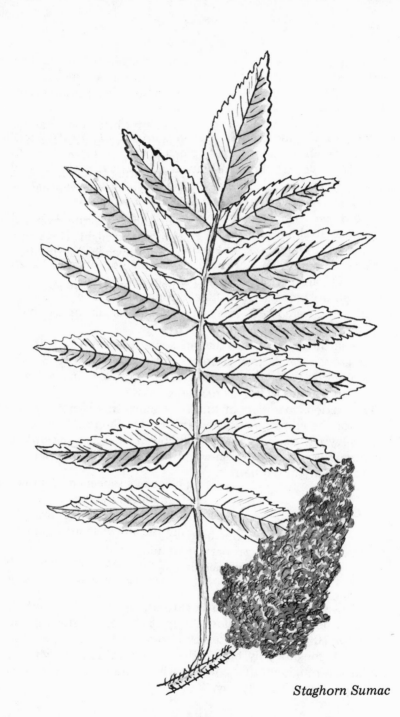

Staghorn Sumac

SUMAC
(Rhus sp.)

Commonly known as the Lemonade Tree as the red berry clusters are used to make a very pleasing but tart drink. Smooth Sumac *(R. glabra)*, Fragrant Sumac *(R. canadensis)* and Red Lemon Berry *(R. integrifolia)* are all large shrubs that produce large clusters of red berries that yield a tart, lemon flavor.

The Staghorn Sumac *(R. typhina)* is perhaps the largest of the genus, attaining a height of 20–30 feet. The young twigs are covered with a fine fuzz, whereas in the other species, the fuzzy hairs are absent. The leaves are all compound, pinnate, 11–29 leaflets, oblong, dark green with pale undersides.

The shrub blooms from June through July. The clusters of berries are covered with fine red hairs and remain on the bush until early spring.

This shrub grows in soils that are somewhat sandy and dry. It has a growth range from Georgia northward to Nova Scotia. Sumac can be found growing in abandoned fields, thickets, and woodland margins as well as roadsides.

The noxious members of the *Rhus* genus should not be mistaken for the edible ones. They are: Poison Sumac *(R. vernix)*, Poison Ivy *(R. toxicodendion)* and Poison Oak *(R. quercifolia)*. All have clusters of greenish-white berries. The edible Sumacs all produce bright red berries.

Sumac Jelly

> 4–6 clusters of ripe berries
> 1 cup of sugar per cup of juice
> 3 ounces liquid pectin

Collect 4–6 clusters of the bright red, ripe fruit. Place into 2 quarts of boiling water. Allow the fruit clusters to steep in the water for 10–15 minutes. Remove from the heat and strain the infusion through a jelly bag. If the color is not red enough, run the juice through another cooking with more fresh picked fruit and strain through a jelly bag.

Measure the juice, place into a saucepan, combine 1 cup of granulated sugar to each cup of hot juice. Mix thoroughly and bring to a boil. Add 3 ounces of liquid pectin. Bring to a boil for 1 full minute. Pour into hot, sterile jelly jars and seal.

Sumac Herb Jelly

Follow the above recipe for Sumac Jelly, and just before you add the liquid pectin, pass a selected herb through the boiling mixture. When the desired flavor and aroma is reached, remove the herb, add pectin and proceed from there.

Sumac Tisane

Select 4 clusters of fully ripened red fruit. Place them into 2 quarts of boiling water. Allow the fruit clusters to steep in the water for 10 minutes.

Remove from the heat and strain, removing all of the fruit and debris. Serve the beverage hot, chilled or on the rocks. Depending on your taste, you may add any desired amount of sugar. The brew will have a delicious lemon flavor.

Thorn Apple

THORN APPLE
(Crataegus sp.)

Scattered throughout eastern portions of Canada and the United States are some 20 or more species of *Crataegus*, the so-called Thorn Apple. There are hundreds of local names, such as Hawthorn, Haw Apples, Rose Apples, etc.

A small tree or large shrub, the Thorn Apple attains heights of 15–20 feet. It is easily recognized because of the plentiful crooked thorns on the branches. The leaves are simple. lobed, and the margins are highly serrated.

The fruit resembles a miniature apple, similar to a Crab Apple, ranging in size from ½ inch to 1 inch. The color varies from yellow to red and generally matures in September or early October. There are 1–5 nutlets as seeds, with a pulpy outer flesh which is quite flavorsome when raw, but much tastier when cooked. In some species the flesh is bitter and no amount of cooking seems to improve the palatability.

Thorn Apple Jelly

> 5 lbs. ripe fruit
> 8 cups sugar
> 5 cups of water
> 3 ounces liquid pectin

Select 5 pounds of fully ripened thorn apples. If possible, it is advisable to have ½ pound of the fruit partially ripened to enhance the flavor and increase the amount of pectin.

Cut the fruit into thin slices, place into a saucepan with 5 cups of cold water, bring to a boil then simmer for 10 minutes. Mash with a hand masher, then allow the pulp to simmer for another 5 minutes.

Remove from the heat and strain through a jelly bag. Gently squeeze out the juice; do not force any of the pulp through the cloth. Save the pulp to make a delicious Thorn Apple Butter. Measure the hot juice, recovering 8 cups. Place into a saucepan and combine 8 cups of granulated sugar. Mix thoroughly and cook over a moderate heat for 3 minutes. Bring to a boil, add 3 ounces of liquid pectin, and hold at a boil for 1 full minute. Skim the surface. Pour into hot, sterile jelly jars and seal.

Spiced Thorn Apple Jelly

        5 lbs. ripe fruit
        5 cups of water
        8 cups of sugar
            Spices: 8 whole cloves
                      1 teaspoon ground allspice
                      2 2-inch sticks of cinnamon
                      1-inch square of whole ginger
        3 ounces liquid pectin

Select 5 pounds of ripened thorn apples. Remove the flower remnants and stems. Cut into thin slices. Place into a saucepan with 5 cups of cold water and add the spice bag. Bring the mixture to a boil then cook at a simmer for 10 minutes. Remove the spice bag and crush the fruit with a potato masher. Strain the juicy pulp through a jelly bag.

Place the hot juice into a saucepan, add 8 cups of granulated sugar, mix thoroughly and bring to a boil. Hold at a boil for 3 minutes, stirring constantly to prevent bottom burn. Add 3 ounces of liquid pectin, hold at a boil for 1 full minute. Skim the surface, pour the jelly into hot, sterile jelly jars and seal.

Thorn Apple Marmalade

        2 quarts ripe thorn apples
        2 medium oranges
        1 medium lemon
        1 cup of cold water
        8 cups of sugar
        3 ounces of liquid pectin

Remove the skins from 2 medium sized oranges, preferably navel oranges, and 1 medium sized lemon. The skins should be peeled in quarters, removing most of the inside white pulp. Chop the rinds into small pieces. Place the chopped rinds into a saucepan, add 1 cup of cold tap water and bring to a boil. Simmer for 20 minutes, stirring occasionally.

Wash, stem, and remove the blossom remnants from 2 quarts of fully ripened thorn apples. Place into the saucepan with the fruit rinds.

Chop the peeled oranges and lemon, remove the seeds and add to the fruit mix. Simmer the mixture for 10 minutes.

Add 8 cups of granulated sugar and bring to a boil. Mix thoroughly. Add 3 ounces of liquid pectin, bring to a boil for 1 full minute. Remove from the heat, skim the surface, pour into hot, sterile jelly jars and seal.

Thorn Apple Pickles

    3 lbs. of fruit
    6 cups of sugar
    ¾ cup of cider vinegar
    1½ cup of water
        Spices: 4 tablespoons of whole cloves
                 ½ stick of cinnamon

Wash thoroughly 3 pounds of fully ripened thorn apples, but do not remove the stems. Make up a syrup of 6 cups of granulated sugar, ¾ cup of cider vinegar, 1½ cups of cold tap water, and bring to a boil. Add the spices, fruit, mix thoroughly and bring to a boil. Cook until fruit is tender.

Pack the fruit into hot, sterile jars. Cook the syrup until thickening occurs and cover the fruit. Seal. Do not serve for about one month. This will allow the spices a chance to work.

Spiced Thorn Apple Butter

    5 lbs. of ripe fruit
    6 cups of sugar
    1 cup of cider vinegar
        Spices: ½ teaspoon of ground cinnamon
                 ½ teaspoon of ground allspice

Wash, stem and remove the flower ends of 5 pounds of fully ripened thorn apples. Cut the little apples into quarters, place into a saucepan, add a little cooking water and bring to a boil. Allow to simmer until soft. Crush with a potato masher and strain through a food mill. This will remove the skins and seeds. If you have leftover fruit pulp, use it in place of new pulp.

181

Place the pulp into a stainless steel or glass saucepan. Add 6 cups of granulated sugar, 1 cup of cider vinegar and mix thoroughly. Add the spices, mix thoroughly, and spoon the spicy pulp into a baking pan. Place in the oven and bake for 4 hours at 250°F. Occasionally stir the mix. When the juice can no longer be separated from the pulp, the butter is finished.

Remove from the oven and spoon into hot, sterile jars and seal. The thorn apple butter can be used immediately. The amount of sugar needed to sweeten the pulp depends on your taste. Therefore adjust accordingly.

Violets

VIOLET
(Viola sp.)

Many of the Violets found growing in the wild are edible; more are poisonous. Some are too fuzzy or bitter to eat. The Wild Sweet Violet *(V. blanda)* also known as the White Violet, is an outstanding potherb. A very attractive flower, the Violet can be found growing in a large variety of environments. It thrives in cool, moist, shaded places, where competition is lessened.

Generally speaking, a small plant of 6–10 inches, Violets are highly branched, slender and produce a great many horizontal runners. The leaves are on long petioles, heart-shaped and range up to 3–4 inches in width. A fragrant flower is produced and is quite edible.

Early Blue Violet or Johnny-jump-up *(V. palmata)* has long been called Wild Okra and is used to thicken soups. The roots and the stem of the Violet is edible and has served as a food source for several hundred years. The leaves are dried and used as a source for an excellent tea. The flowers of all the Violets can be used to make fine jellies.

Violet Jelly

> 1 pint of flowers
> Juice of ½ lemon
> 2 cups of sugar per cup of juice
> 3 ounces of liquid pectin

Collect enough violet flowers to fill a pint jar. Stuff the jar with as many flowers as possible. Cover the blossoms with boiling water and cover. Keep out of the bright sunshine and other bright lights. Allow the mixture to sit for 24 hours. This will draw the color and sugar from the blossoms into the solution.

Strain the infusion through a jelly bag, removing the blossoms and debris. Place the juice in a saucepan. Add the juice of ½ lemon and mix thoroughly. The lemon juice will reduce the color of the violet infusion. Bring the mixture to a boil for 1 minute. Add 2 cups of sugar to each cup of the infusion and 3 ounces of liquid pectin. Hold at a hard boil for 1 full minute. Skim the surface, pour into hot, sterile jelly jars and seal.

184

Violet-Crab Apple Jelly

    1 pint violet flowers
6—8 partially ripe crab apples
    2 cups of sugar per cup of juice
    3 ounces liquid pectin

Fill a pint jar completely with violet flowers. The more flowers you collect, the stronger the flavor and color. Cover the blossoms with boiling water and cover. Keep out of bright sunlight and other bright lights. Allow to stand for 24 hours. This will draw out into solution the color and sugars.

The next day, core and remove the blossom remnants for 6—8 partially ripened crab apples. Cut into quarters, place into a saucepan and cook over a moderate heat until soft. Then mash with a potato masher.

Strain the crab apple sauce through a jelly bag. Combine the apple juice with the violet infusion. Bring the mixture to a boil for 1 full minute. Add 2 cups of granulated sugar to each cup of juice. Bring to a hard boil for 1 full minute.

Remove from the heat, skim the surface, pour into hot, sterile jelly jars and seal.

Spiced Violet Jelly

    4 quarts of violet flowers
    ½ cup of white vinegar
    ¼ cup of water
    5 cups of sugar
    3 ounces liquid pectin
    Spices: 6 whole cloves
              1 tablespoon ground cinnamon
              1 teaspoon ground allspice

Collect and lightly wash 4 quarts of violet flowers. Place them into a large pyrex type jar and cover with boiling water. Keep the infusion out of bright sunlight and allow to sit overnight for 24 hours. The next day, strain the infusion through a jelly bag to remove all debris.

Into a saucepan combine ½ cup of white vinegar, ¼ cup of water, 5 cups of sugar and the spices. Mix thoroughly, place over a low heat and cook for 10 minutes. Stir the mixture occasionally. Then strain the mixture through a fine sieve.

Combine the flower infusion and the spicy syrup, bring to a boil, add 3 ounces of liquid pectin and boil for 1 full minute. Pour into hot, sterile jelly jars and seal.

Johnny-jump-up Jelly

> 1 cup of flowers
> 1 cup of sugar
> 3—4 crab apples

Johnny-jump-ups are violets that produce a flower that resembles a pansy. They do not grow in great abundance. Collect 1 cup full, as stuffed as you can get it. Place the flowers into a heat resistant jar, cover with boiling water, cover and place in a dark place, away from bright light. Allow to stand for 24 hours.

Next day, strain the infusion, removing blossoms and other debris. Peel a few partially ripened crab apples and cook for 10 minutes in a little water. Strain, recover the juice. This will provide a little flavor plus pectin. Combine the two juices, bring to a boil for 1 full minute. Add 1 cup of granulated sugar, mix thoroughly and boil for 1 full minute. Skim the surface, pour into hot sterile jelly jars and seal.

Violet Herb Jelly

> 1 pint violet flowers
> 2 cups of sugar per cup of juice
> 3 ounces of liquid pectin
> Selected herb

Read one of the recipes on how to prepare violet jelly. Add the 3 ounces of liquid pectin and boil for 1 full minute. Bruise the leaves of a selected freshly picked herb(s), tie in a small bunch, hold the stem ends and pass the bruised leaves through the hot juice. Do this until you achieve the desired strength of flavoring. You may also add a vegetable food coloring at this point. Bring to a boil once again. Remove from the heat, skim the surface, pour into hot, sterile jelly jars and seal.

186

You may use such herbs as: basil, thyme, mint, tarragon, horehound, peppermint or sage. If fresh materials are used, the herb should be suspended in the hot juice mixture. If prepared herbs are used, you may find that a spice bag will be necessary. This will keep the loose material from filtering throughout the juice.

Virginia Creeper

VIRGINIA CREEPER
(Parthenocissus quinquefolia)

A woody vine that is more often than not mistaken by many individuals for Poison Ivy. It is well known by several different names, among them: Tree Creeper, Woodbine, Virginia Woodbine, Creeper Vine and of course Virginia Creeper.

A climbing vine, it attains heights or lengths to over 20 feet. It has tendrils located along the woody vine that have adhesive discs that allow it to adhere to almost anything.

The leaves alternate on the vine, compound with usually 5 leaflets, but may vary from 3–7. The leaflets radiate from a common point, oblong with toothed margins. The flowers are greenish in color and in loose clusters. These flowers yield blue colored small berries, red stemmed, and bear in the early fall. They can be eaten raw or cooked in jellies.

This beautiful climbing vine has a growth range from Florida north to Quebec and west to Texas and Saskatchewan. There are about a dozen related species in North America and all bear edible fruit.

Virginia Creeper Jelly

> 1 quart ripe berries
> 1 cup of sugar per cup of juice
> 3 ounces liquid pectin

Gather only fully ripe berries, as green ones are too bitter. Wash and stem 1 quart of berries. Place into a saucepan, cover the bottom with a little water and cook until all the fruit pops its skins. Strain through a jelly bag. Recover the juice and measure.

Combine 1 cup of granulated sugar with each cup of juice in a saucepan, and boil until the sugar completely dissolves. Stir constantly. Add 3 ounces of liquid pectin and boil for 1 full minute. Skim off the colorful foam, pour into hot, sterile jelly jars and seal.

Virginia Creeper Jam

    1 quart of ripe berries
    1 cup of sugar per cup of pulp
    3 ounces liquid pectin

Stem and wash 1 quart of fully ripened berries. Place into a saucepan with a little cooking water. Cook until all the berries pop their skins.

Strain the hot berries and juice through a food mill. Recover the hot juicy pulp and measure. Combine each cup of juicy pulp with a cup of granulated sugar. Bring to a boil. Add 3 ounces of liquid pectin. Hold at a boil for 1 full minute.

Skim off the colorful foam, pour into hot, sterile jelly jars and seal.

Wintergreen

WINTERGREEN
(Gaultheria procumbens)

This little taste treasure is known by many common or local names, among them: Checkerberry, Teaberry, and Boxberry. It is common to shaded, moist woodlands. A small shrubby plant, it attains heights to 3–6 inches and generally grows in thick plantings.

The leaves are evergreen, tasty, aromatic, in clusters at the top of the stem, which arises from an underground rhizome. The leaves are thick, stiff, crisp, dark green or red with a lighter underside. The leaves contain oil of wintergreen, hence its aromatic aroma, flavor and name.

The white bell-shaped flower yields a fleshy berry-like fruit. The red fruit can be found on the plant from August throughout the winter and spring, unless the birds get there first.

Wintergreen has a growth range from Georgia north to Newfoundland.

Wintergreen Jelly

> 1 pint of fresh picked leaves
> 1 pint of ripe berries
> 1 quart of water
> 1 cup of sugar per cup of juice
> 3 ounces liquid pectin

Wash and discard any bad leaves, bruise all leaves, place into a saucepan with 1 pint of cold water. Bring to a boil and simmer for 15 minutes. This will free much of the oil of wintergreen from the bruised leaves.

In a separate saucepan, combine 1 pint of ripe berries and 1 pint of cold tap water. Bring to a boil. Simmer until berries soften, then crush with a potato masher. Drain the hot juicy, aromatic pulp through a jelly bag.

Strain the leaf infusion, combine with the berry juice and 1 cup of sugar to each cup of juice in a saucepan. Bring to a boil, add 3 ounces of liquid pectin and hold at a boil for 1 full minute. Remove, skim the surface, pour into hot sterile jelly jars and seal.